Herbert Remmel

Operation Shamrock

From Cologne to Ballinlough

A German and Irish
boyhood in World War II
and post war years
1946 – 1949

Aubane
Historical
Society

Aubane
Millstreet
County Cork

2009

Title of German edition:
Operation Shamrock – Eine deutsch-irische Nachkriegskindheit

Index
Photos: WWII Multimedia Database (2); Alan Persse, Dublin (1); St. Michael Oblate Parish, Inchicore (1); miksch architects, Düsseldorf (2); Bunkerarchäologie Köln (1); Irish Red Cross Society (1); Dermot Coyle, Castlebellingham (1); O'Connel Family, Cork (3); Muckross House (1) private

Copyright 2009 English edition:
Aubane Historical Society, Angela Clifford, Herbert Remmel
English translation: Angela Clifford
Cover design & Layout: Helmut Sander
Aubane Historical Society
ISBN: 978-1-903497-53-1
Orders: jacklaneaubane@hotmail.com
htp://aubanehistoricalsociety.org

Introduction

This is a refreshingly unusual book. It is mainly about rural Ireland in the 1940s and it is full of fun, enjoyment, insights and sheer delight in everything about that society.

Unusual because according to all things literary this is not how things were. To the current literary mindset such a place in such a period should not exist and instead we should only be reading of variations on the "squinting windows" theme at best – and more usually descriptions of various forms of awfulness for mind and body and hints of even worse. Dire is the only word for it.

But this author has no axe to grind, no agenda to follow. His objectivity derives from the fact that he was an outsider who found himself in the middle of the society and writes straightforwardly about what he experienced and the impressions made on him, and writes with a great talent for vividly painting a variety of people and situations in a few sentences.

Herbert Remmel was one of the German children who was brought to Ireland after World War II by the Red Cross. His book begins with wartime life in Cologne and there is a graphic description of War and everyday life in a suburb of Cologne and further afield as experienced by a small child, his family and neighbours.

When he writes about Ireland he passes casual comments on the distinctive characteristics of Irish society to which our literati seem totally oblivious, comments which speak volumes for his incisiveness. For example when referring to "his" Irish grandmother's dress he says: "But Granny didn't only wear black in grief: it was a sort of traditional wear for older ladies. It certainly wasn't peasant-wear for there never were any in Ireland. The British had seen to that in their colonial days. They would only tolerate the existence of poor tenants, not peasants with land and property rights." (page 144)

No peasants in Ireland! Never!

He is perfectly correct – and it is the key to understanding rural Ireland. Ireland went from dispossessed, rootless and free Gaelic clansmen to independent farmers and missed out on feudalism and peasant life. A peasantry and their rulers have an organic, interdependent relationship.

The Gaelic clansmen were broken off and detached from their Gaelic way of life by war, conquest and confiscation. There was no human relationship established between the destroyers – the new rulers – and the destroyed. There was no common bond. The only links were those of legalised terror and humiliation. The clansmen to be free had to be lawless. The bottom and top ends of society were at loggerheads, permanently. There was no symbiotic relationship between the two. It was not a peasant/lord relationship.

Herbert Remmell's book does not go into such abstruse matters. It is a child's eye view of Ireland as he found it just after the War, and as such is a joy to read and a great release from the dogmas about rural Ireland. It makes one want to invite more Germans here to spend some time and write about us because to paraphrase Kipling they would hopefully, like Herbert, come to know Ireland well because they more than Ireland know.

Jack Lane
Aubane Historical Society
January 2008

A Word Before Starting

On the afternoon of 27th July 1946 the Liverpool mail-boat docked at Dun Laoghaire. About 60 German children disembarked. That day marks the beginning of my 'Irish biography', which I have set down on its 60th anniversary, mainly for my children.

At the end of 1945 the Irish Red Cross launched a project to help war-children, called Operation Shamrock. The idea was to bring German children to stay with Irish families for three years. Aged nine, I was one of those lucky children who embarked from a demoralised and starving Germany, lying in ruins, to arrive in a different world, a land at peace and with a totally different way of life.

My nearly three years with the Irish were amongst the happiest and most interesting of my childhood. Down the years I have told stories about my Irish experiences to my children, family, and friends, and they started pressurising me to set down my 'Irish biography' in sequence. This I have done without literary pretensions, seeking to retain the child's view of events, and I have added an account of my childhood before my Irish adventure.

Now, under pressure from my Irish friends, I have been prevailed upon to allow an English edition of my memoir, to which I have added a few more recollections.

Pinnow,
January 2008

NOTES: I have added some footnotes which may interest readers. In particular I have given some of the Cologne dialect 'Koelsch Platt' words in use. Readers may notice that Koelsch Platt is very different to standard German!

1

Prologue

On this Summer's day we were turning the hay on the lower meadow on Tawny Lake. It was hot, and the monotonous work had tired me. Eugene and I had already turned nearly half the swathes of hay, breaking up the long rows of mown grass with our wooden hay-rakes. The meadow rose gently from the lake and, as I finished my row at the upper end, I turned to start on the next swathe down towards the lake.

While turning, I must have caught it in the corner of my eye, the silver point in the summer-blue sky: obviously a four-engine bomber; height 6,000 to 7,000 metres. Carefully keeping my eye on the dot, and slightly leaning on my rake, I let myself down onto the unturned grass. Lying on my back, arms folded behind my head, I watched the sky, waiting. Any moment now, black clouds of smoke from *Flak*-shells would be framing the tiny silver fish up there. But that same moment I realised that there was no *Flak* here and that the dot up there could be no bomber (*Flak* = **FL**ieger**Ab**-*wehr*-**K**anone = 8,8 cm anti aircraft artillery). Since coming to live here on the Nally Farm in the village of Ballinlough in County Mayo, I'd scarcely thought of my home far away in Cologne. And when I did it was because something around me sparked me off, like that silver dot up there in the sky.

*

Despite air-raid warnings, I often used to lie on the *Autobahn* (A 3 to-day) slope in *Höhenhaus* near Cologne with my friends, arms folded behind my head, watching the fleets of incoming US bombers: hundreds of tiny silver fishes, their arrival presaged minutes before by an uncanny deep, vibrating growl. We'd learned to judge when the local *Flak*-batteries on Emberg – which we called 'our' *Flak* – would start firing. Likewise we knew we'd hear the sound of the firing before the shells found their targets in the sky and explode. And we'd also learned that we couldn't wait too long after seeing the first explosion clouds before running and squeezing in under the *Berliner* Road bridge crossing the *Autobahn*. For that was when the dangerous, jagged, *Flak* splinters would come hurtling down.

Yes, us scamps – aged eight, nine, and ten – were well-seasoned 'warriors' by now, at least where aerial warfare was concerned. The B17 (the '*Viermot*' four-engine bomber), the Lightning, the Mustang, the Mosquito – we could reel off the technical data for all of them and, even when they were flying high, we could still identify them. The long, octagonal incendiary bombs were no mystery to us. And we'd felt the effect of a aerial blockbuster bomb (large-scale demolition bomb loaded with approx. 1500 Kg explosives) when one fell in the *Neurath* Housing Estate where we lived: it blew away half an apartment block, destroyed the one next to it, and lifted the roofs of most of the other blocks. Another blockbuster fell in *Sandberg* (sand hill) without detonating. For days it lay in the caretaker's garden and we were made to inspect the "Anglo-American terror weapon" by the Nazi authorities. I can still remember it clearly, lying in a small crater: an elongated barrel made of sheet metal, burst open with a green-yellow gunge oozing out of it.

Flak-splinters, aircraft amunitions and, above all, the plexiglass from the cockpits of shot-down planes, were highly-prized collector's items for us children who lived in the estate. And anyone who could dismantle a bit from a shot-down plane – he was king.

One night an English bomber was shot down and crashed not 50 metres from where we lived. It had already dropped his load of bombs, and it fell straight down, the impact burying its nose on the heights by the sewage plant on *Flachsroster* Way, roughly where St. Hedwig's Church now stands. A wing must have broken off as it fell and, as the wing hit one of the apartment blocks, the petrol tank exploded. Days later the grown-ups were still discussing the agonising death of a man who lived there: for a long, long time he was calling for help in the burning house but couldn't be reached by the firemen.

We shared a cellar with four other families living on our staircase and we'd take shelter there. Just after the plane crashed, my brother Hans rushed out with the other residents, but I was kept back under the eye of cousin Leni as I had mumps or something. I was kept in bed the next day too, while Hans got going on the aircraft wreckage with our friends. Even though it was being guarded by air-raid wardens, Hans was able to dismantle a clock-like device from the instrument-panel which he brought home triumphantly. Hans was king and his little brother was totally envious.

2

Neurath Housing Estate

I was born on the *Neurath* Estate: 2 *Goslar* Way, first staircase, left. A home birth, as befitted a workers' family in 1936. This estate forms part of the Cologne suburb, *Höhenhaus*, just beyond Cologne-*Mülheim* on the right, eastern, bank of the Rhine looking downstream. [1]

The estate was part of a new socialised housing development in the 1920s and 1930s. [2] Originally planned as emergency, short-term, housing, it was later expanded into a huge project providing basic accommodation. The most simple building techniques were used: long terraces of two-storied apartment blocks, each with eight entrances, were erected – but they had a human dimension. This came about because they started by building full-size lathe and cardboard models of two half-blocks. These must have met expectations.

One of the Neurath housing blocks

There was plenty of space between the blocks, enough for each of the four families sharing an entrance to have a bleaching-green, a few square metres of garden and a cherry tree. There were two attic-rooms for each entrance, which were supplied with water but had no toilet.

The flats stretched to the left and right of *Bode* Street, to which they were linked by lanes, each called after a place in the *Harz* (*Harz* = mountainous region in Saxony-*Anhalt* and Lower Saxony). At the beginning of *Bode* Street there was a single-storied service area (a co-op), in which there were bakers, a dairy, and butchers. There were more small shops on the gable-ends of the apartment blocks.

An expanse of ground, on which there was a children's play-area with sand-boxes and a kindergarden, separated the two halves of the northern terrace-block. Later a pond was added to provide water in case of fire: I nearly drowned in it, aged about five. Loni Krupp, a young girl from our flats, rescued me and saved my life with resuscitation, for I'd already lost consciousness.

One of the two sewage stations on the estate was situated on *Flachsroster* Way. It treated and pumped away the district waste. *Neurath* Estate is to one side of *Berliner* Street, which connects Cologne and *Mülheim*: it can be approached through *Bode* Street which leads to the centre or, on the south side, by a narrow country path along the allotments [3] by the motorway (*Autobahn*). *Flachsroster* Way, an untarred sandy lane, runs along the

9

northern side of the settlement up to *Schönrath* Farm, passing the gable-end of *Goslarer* Way where we lived. At that time there were allotments along the north side of *Flachsroster* Way. A brewery, *Bergische Löwenbrauerei*, stood slightly apart on the corner of *Berliner* Street and *Flachsroster* Way, dominating the district with its chimneys and the mansion where the owners lived.

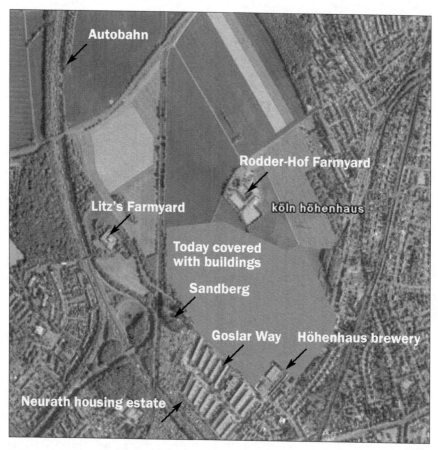

Höhenhaus and Neurath in the 1940s

The Tropon plant was on the edge of *Höhenhaus*, technically part of Mülheim. It mass-produced Tropon, an artificial edible protein.

The plain design of *Neurath* Estate matched the simple life-style of its residents – and their neighbourly warmth. Simple folk were comfortable here: workers who found their living in the industrial areas of Cologne-*Mülheim*, in places like *Carlswerk* – the *Felten & Guilleame* cable factory where father worked – along with *Deutz* Motors, the iron rolling mill *Böcking,* *Liesegang* and others. Here in *Neurath* everyone was more or less equal: pretensions were virtually unknown. People shared the bath-tub in the cellar, as well as the wash-house; and neighbours helped out with an occasional loan of salt, sugar, flour and bread. The only language spoken was Cologne platt [4] – anyone trying to speak High (Standard) German got only pitying smiles, because all they could produce was *"Huhdeutsch met Knubbele"* (Standard German with knots). Outsiders often spoke of *Neurath* as a "poor folks' estate". But in reality it was the milieu of those working families who had the good fortune to escape the dark city backyards. They had the benefit of three-room apartments including a living room/kitchen with built-in pantry and inside toilet; light; and clean air. That – and the open countryside all around – is what made father and mother fight to get our flat allocated to us. They wanted a healthy environment for their children to grow up in.

3

Mother And Father, Oma And Opa [5]

Mother – nee Eva Gross – was born on 20th April 1906, the youngest child of an employee family in the town of *Daun, Eifel* (*Eifel* = mountainous region in the triangle made by the Moselle and Rhine rivers). She had four sisters and a brother. I never met my *Daun* grandparents. *Opa* Franz Gross served on the Eastern Front in the First World War. During an artillery bombardment he was buried in a freezing trench at 25 degrees below zero and it was several hours before he was dug out. Given an invalidity discharge, he never recovered from his injuries and died before the end of the War. Before that he was an employee and by his efforts rose to a good position, ending up as well-master, in charge of water quality, for the mineral water company *"Dauner Sprudel"* (*Daun* Sparkling Water).

After my *Daun Oma* died in the early 1920s there was nothing to hold my mother in the place and she followed her two sisters, Barbara (Auntie Bäb) and Hedwig (Auntie Hed) to Cologne. Both of her other sisters, Aunts Dina and Maria, had married American GIs, who were briefly stationed as occupation troops in the *Eifel* at the end of the First World War, and gone to live in the USA. Mother's brother Nikolaus (Uncle Klöös) had found work in the lignite coalfields near Cologne.

11

Mother attended National School in *Daun*, but got no training position. Like her sisters she'd got no chance of further education because of family financial circumstances. In Cologne she worked in the *Felten & Guilleame* Cable Works as a cable-finisher.

My Father – Christian Remmel – was born on 15th September 1904 in the *Mülheim* district of Cologne. His background was working class as well. He had a sister, Aunt Grete, and a brother, Uncle Willi; two other brothers had died in the first year of infancy. His parents were also of modest circumstances: Oma Gertrud (b. 1874) and Opa Johann (b. 1871). Oma's father, Johann Eudenbach, was a cobbler in *Refrath* (near Cologne); Opa's father was a day-labourer in *Schweinheim*, a village which has since become a suburb of the *Dellbrück* area of Cologne. Before Oma married, she was a housemaid and then a cook in 'gentry' houses.

Grandfather Franz Gross (seated) as soldier in WW I

Opa's father died young and family rumour has it that his wife, my great-grandmother, suffered from religious mania and wanted Opa to become a priest. So she guarded him from worldly sin and kept him away from school as much as possible. But, still under-age, Grandpa Johann bunked off to Cologne where he found work. One of his jobs was foundry-finisher in the *Deutz* motor works.

Because he was kept out of school, Opa was nearly illiterate. He joined the Social Democrats while he was still in his teens, attended their Worker Education Associations diligently and learned not only how to read and write but attained considerable learning. In 1914, when the Social Democrats voted the war-credits in the *Reichstag*, Opa Johann left the Party, loudly protesting this betrayal of the ideals of Social Democracy, and he never returned.

Opa Johann was somehow drawn into the military in 1890 and stationed in the Cuirassier-Barracks in the *Deutz* area of Cologne. Though proud to be in the barracks where Wilhelm Liebknecht (early leader of the German

My mother with her mother
Magdalena Gross, nee Maus

Grandma and grandfather Gertrud
and Johann Remmel

Social Democrats) was born, he hated the Prussian military like the plague. Using a razor and a nicotine concoction, he carefully nurtured up a lurid boil on his neck which would never heal, eventually securing his discharge.

Oma and Opa Remmel loved us children and were really jolly grandparents. Opa was a real buddy – you could get up to mischief with him. But he was also worldly-wise and had countless sayings, such as: 'since death came into fashion, one can no longer be sure of life', or 'Beware of parochial parsons in politics'. Father too was only able to attend National School (*Volksschule*): in *Mülheim*. Like his own father he was to acquire wider scholarship in night-schools – including learning Esperanto [6].

He joined the Labour Esperanto Association and participated in its international rally in London in the 1930s. He was the first member of our family to travel abroad. Father was also a passionate listener to the radio and he'd often tell me how he'd bought a receiver out of his first wage, a simple crystal set as it was then. Later he got a fantastic receiver, made by his favourite manufacturer, Loewe. I remember the magic eye of the *Loewe-Opta* radio, which lit up green or faded as the needle was tuned fan-wise.

13

Father never learned a trade. He worked as a casual labourer in the AKLA Leather Works in the *Bucheim* district of Cologne, or on building sites. From around 1926 he was first a warehouseman and then delivery-man for the provision merchants, Schmitz, in *Dellbrück* district of Cologne. Father liked to tell us about his time there, driving what was then a three-ton HGV with his deliveryman: they'd negotiate the bumpy roads into the Bergish land district to deliver goods. The lorry tarpaulin was embellished with the great advertising slogan, "Ladies' Solace Coffee" [7]. The farmers used to say: "The two Casanovas are coming".

In 1933 the Nazis forced Schmitz, the owner, to dismiss father on the grounds that he belonged to the KPD (Communist Party of Germany). He then got a job in *Felten & Guilleaume* Company in *Mülheim*. Father took up politics early in life, as did his sister and brother, possibly influenced by Opa but certainly because they were growing up in the Weimar Republic era. He joined the Young Communist League in 1922 and the KPD [8] itself in 1925. His sister Gertrud (Auntie Gret) and brother Willi followed suit. When the Party was forced into illegality in 1933, after the Nazis took power, Father became one of those who took care of party members eva-ding the authorities. At first his job was to look after and assist the Party comrades living as outlaws, on the run from the *Gestapo*, and to help them get across the Border to safety. Later, when anti-fascist work could only be undertaken by small cells of three, father brought the emigrants to safety using unmarked crossings between Belgium and Holland. This was done with his friend, Heinrich Dachtler, who had a heavy American motor-bike and side-car (trademark: Indian). By this time they were helping not only their Communist comrades, but also others in a perilous position who had to flee Nazi-Germany on political or racial grounds, including Jews. Father was also able to help get his own brother, my Uncle Willi, to Holland in 1935. A year later Uncle Willi left Holland for Spain, a volunteer to the Inter-national Brigade (*Ernst-Thälmann-Battalion*). He fought to defend the legal Republic against the Franco-putschists, with their Nazi-German abettors in the Condor Legion, and was wounded three times. Between 1939 and April 1945 Uncle Willi was to suffer in the Nazi Concentration Camps, *Sachsenhau-sen*, *Buchenwald*, and *Mauthausen* where he was liberated by the Red Army.

Father and Mother married on 9th December 1933. Although both of them worked for the same company, they met at a kiosk across the junction of *Keup* Street with *Gladbacher* Street in *Mülheim*. In 1997 mother was still able to show me the spot and tell me the touching story of how they got to know each other. The kiosk, at any rate, is still there.

My brother Hans was born in 1935, the same year that my parents succeeded in getting a home allocated to them on the *Neurath* Estate. My father was particularly glad to move into this area, where he was surroun-ded by his friends and comrades.

My father (right) as a deliveryman for a Cologne merchant house

Immediately after seizing power, the Nazis launched an assault on this worker-milieu in *Neurath*. And indeed the district was full of Social Democrats and Communists, which is why it was known as the 'Red District', and even 'Little Moscow'.

In later years my father told me how the Nazis, shortly after taking power, stormed the district, sealed off *Bode* Street, and collected all known Social Democrats and Communists from their homes. There were

Hans and me with mother ...

... and with father at the end 1930s

Riding the poor man's horse

flocks of them and they were brought to the exhibition area in *Deutz*, later a sub-section of the KZ [9] or to the El-De building in Cologne, the seat of the *Gestapo* [10].

It was days, weeks, or months later before most of them got back to their families. They'd been interrogated and many were tortured. Some never returned. And we were often told the story of the three resistance fighters who'd hidden in the cellars of one of the apartment blocks but were betrayed. The Nazi police besieged the place for hours. There was an exchange of fire in which a police officer lost his life. The cellar was stormed and the three resistance people cut down. Then, as a horrible warning, their shot-up bodies were left lying on the pavement of Bode Street for a long time.

Journey into the blue with Toni the neighbour. Toni, just 18, was called up to the army and he was killed in action in Poland on first day of WW II

4

Games: Marbles And Foil-Strips

Long after *Höhenhaus* was incorporated into Cologne in 1914, there were fields and pastures belonging to three farms to the west of *Berliner* Street. This was where the non-profitmaking Workers' Housing Cooperative built *Neurath* Estate in 1931-2. It took its name from *Neurath* Farm, which has now completely disappeared.

Schönrath Farm lay directly behind the estate, only separated from it by the *Sandberg* (Sand Hill), the Cologne-*Mülheim-Düsseldorf* railtrack, and a paddock. The Litz family, known throughout Europe for breeding draught-horses, had owned this farm for generations, and so the place was always only known as "the Litz farmyard". Adjoining the farm was an ancient forest of mighty trees called the *Litze Bösch*. In 1935 a swathe was cut through the *Litze Bösch* by the *Reichs*-Motorway to build what is *Autobahn* No. 3 today; Adolf Hitler appeared in person to open this first section of the *Autobahn*: no-one in *Neurath* took much notice. The Rodder Farm was also on the edge of *Höhenhaus*, in the *Emberg* district, but it was surrounded by plough-land and was therefore of not much interest to us children.

My favourite playgrounds at the time were the *Litze Bösch*; *Sandberg;* the immediately adjacent level crossing at *Flachsroster* Way, with its signalman's hut and alarm; and the then half-completed Cologne-*Mühlheim* motorway exit road – that is, when I wasn't roaming the estate with my friends.

Then, beside the Tropon Works, there was Fort XI b, which formed part of the defences built around Cologne in 1870. In fact, it was only a minor casemat fort, built to link up with other fortifications, but to us it was an adventure-playground. In the 1920s its foreground was turned into a green park in one of the work-creation schemes. It was also the terminus, with a turning loop, of the No. 2 Tramline.

Us children were never at a loss for games and ideas for games. We loved playing marbles. Using the heel of our shoes, we'd grind small round pits into the earth into which the beautiful, multi-coloured glass marbles were rolled from a prescribed distance.

Using a stick, and making plenty of noise, we drove old bicycle wheel-rims, all the spokes missing, through the estate. In the Autumn we cobbled up tin smoke-boxes – empty food tins, holed and threaded with a wire loop. Filled with dry foliage, lit, and whizzed round by the loops, we covered many an estate-path with thick smoke. Then came the great spectacle of housewives rushing out to save their clean white washing, – lying on the bleaching-greens, from the smoke attacks.

The Estate paths were at that time boxed in with mulberry-hedges, home to thick fat silk-worms. These luscious, green-shimmering caterpillars had a big spike on their rear which bent forward. Nearly all my playmates had a small box, carton, or something like that, lined with mulberry leaves, for 'his' silk-worms. You can imagine my surprise and despair one day to find that my silk-worm had disappeared from its cigar-box, even though this only had small air-holes. In tears, I took this tragedy to my father. He enlightened me: the caterpillar had turned itself into a chrysalis and I hadn't noticed the spun pupa in the corner of the box, under the leaves.

A more martial game was target practice: armed with knives, daggers, and even screw-drivers, we had to conquer circles drawn out on the ground by setting up 'bridgeheads'. This was done by treating the circles as a target in which our knives had to stick – which turned us into perfect knife-throwers.

Again and again we'd make use of bits and pieces from the war in our games. We cut long thin strips from the inner tubes of tyres from shot-down British or US bombers to make rubber-slings for catapults. The tinfoil strips dropped by Anglo-American planes to deceive German radar made lovely finery for Red Indian warriors, while the 'advance' of aerial warfare granted us children our first experience of boating. American Mustang fighter planes started to escort bomber-fleets deep into Germany and they simply jettisoned their empty auxiliary petrol tanks. Many a father, or older boy, used plate-shears to simply cut rectangular or circular entry openings into the top of these now empty aerodynamically-designed containers – and the canoe was ready. What we children had to learn in practice – in a giant bomb-crater full of ground-water – that the things were devilish hard to handle and liable to capsize. However, once weighed down with sand-bags as ballast, unwanted and dangerous 'Eskimo-rollovers' could generally be avoided.

Of course we played at 'real' war on *Sandberg*, with sticks as guns and empty food-tins as hand-grenades. Somehow Hans had acquired a real French steel helmet and, wearing this, one of us was patrol-leader. Reaching the railway line our patrol was wiped out by 'hostile fire' and we were badly wounded. Our nurses had to bandage and mother us. But when they began to diagnose abdomen wounds and enthusiastically unbuttoned our pants, we started getting distrustful and suddenly recovered. Then, in a spirit of equality, we'd sometimes send one or two female soldiers into hostile fire, after which our deployment as volunteer first-aid men provided deep insights.

But what were the games of these children, playing at war, against the adult 'war games' on land and in the air, the danger of which we only gradually began to realise? In the first instance it was all only something interesting, adventurous, and exciting.

18

5

The Neurath Bunker

One of my most deeply-etched memories is of the building of the high-rise concrete *Bunker* (air shelter) at the end of *Bode*-Street. That must have been in the Winter of 1941-2 when I was five years of age. The *'Führer* Action Order' for *Bunker* Erection was promulgated in October 1940. Opa was the watchman on the *Bunker* building-site.

At this time he was employed by a security company (*Wach- und Schließgesellschaft*), wore a dark-blue uniform, a cap with two crossed keys in place of a cockade, and a giant pistol-holster on his belt – with contents. Opa and Oma lived on 2 *Goslarer* Way, in the attic-flat above us. When Opa was in high spirits and wanted to give Grandma a fright, he'd pull out this pistol, probably a *Parabellum* 08. Every time Oma would shriek out: "Johann, stop that, it's dangerous!". But Opa would give us grandsons a confidential wink: he'd told us his pistol wasn't loaded with real bullets, only blanks. At any rate at twilight Opa would be sitting in his watchman's hut on the *Bunker* building-site. (There was no flood-light work because of the British bombers.) For a while he'd keep the coke fire left by the workers going in its brazier. We children were let heat up bits of scrap iron rods until they'd glow red-hot and then thrust them into the snow, which made a wonderful hissing sound.

In May 1942 there was the first British large-scale attack on Cologne – the first 1000-bomber raid on a German city. [11] The *Bunker* had just been finished, but not quite: you had to go up a wooden ramp to get in. After the attack and all-clear, we were able to leave and found pieces of paper were whirling down from the heavens. I remember my mother picking one of them up (the bill of an *Ehrenfeld* company) and saying: "Oh, dear God, *Ehrenfeld* is falling on us". The hot air rising from the flaming inferno of Cologne had carried paper for twelve kilometres (as the crow flies), from the Cologne *Ehrenfeld* district on the far side of the Rhine to *Höhenhaus*.

As for the *Bunker*: over the years it became a second home, not only for families from the *Neurath* Estate, but later also for bombed-out families from Cologne, particularly from *Mülheim*.

In our family each of us had by our bed a small alarm-suitcase, or a box tied with string, with the most necessary utensils, ready to be grabbed. Then, if during the night the shrill undulating tone of the air-raid siren went off, we'd crawl out of our beds, get dressed still half-asleep, hurry out

Neurath air raid shelter (Bunker) with park-like-greenery at the front

into the night, pitch-dark because of the black-out regulations, and make our way to the *Bunker*. I'll never forget the eerie scene on the estate paths and on *Bode* Street: hundreds of people running, stumbling, and feeling their way along the street; some grumbling quietly, others cursing and some even laughing, if you inadvertently bumped into someone: "Oh dear God, Mrs. Trimborn, it's you" [12]. "Yes, Mrs. Remmel, and next time I'll stick a cat's eye on my backside" [13]. One night we slept right through the preliminary and full alarms, so we were late rising from the feathers. As we ran to the *Bunker*, the British bombers could already be heard rumbling overhead, along with the barking discharge of the *Flak*. We stood by the *Bunker* transfixed, looking across the allotments towards *Emberg*. From here bright cones thrown by the searchlights had pin-pointed the apex of the bomber-fleet and 'our' *Flak* was spewing a raging barrage from every barrel. With every shot, the barrels spat out metre-long snakes of flame, for split seconds bathing the area in a fascinating light. We were lucky: the *Bunker*-warden was just closing the great steel door. He just about let us in, grumbling all the while. A minute later and the iron law would have kept us out: once the *Bunker* door is closed after a full alarm, it's not re-opened, not even for panic-stricken people hammering on it, desperate for a place of safety. Horribly beautiful too were the 'Christmas Trees', which often hovered over Cologne for several minutes during the night alarms, marking out the target areas for the bombers to aim at.

Inside the *Bunker* we shared a windowless cell with others. With several wooden two-tier bunk beds, there was barely room to stand. The air was bad, what with the emanations from the concrete and the people. And soon the *Bunker* was infested with bed-bugs, so there was the added smell of the insecticide regularly sprayed from spray-guns – to no effect. In the end we had recourse to extreme measures: all the wooden beds were carried out and burned. But the respite was brief. When the light was turned on, the columns of bugs could be seen moving along the bed-posts. Then the call came for bug-cracking. They smelt terrible, and the bug-bites always grew into big irritable spots. During air-raids the *Bunker* sheltered all the locals and more; and the passageways, anteroom and stairs were always a hive of excited and noisy activity: children rushing around yelling, grown-ups giving out, and many a neighbourly row being resumed.

If bombs were dropped during a raid, the NSV, [14] even before the all-clear was sounded, would set up long tables in the turning loop of *Bode* Street, laden with slices of thickly-buttered slices of bread and salami. And there'd often be coffee made with beans – that is, real coffee, not gnat's piss,[15] as the substitute coffee (*Ersatzkaffee*) made of chicory or barley was known. You could help yourself, free of charge. Popular morale had to be maintained. This service was provided in central Cologne, *Mülheim*, or on occasion *Höhenhaus* – but this good life did not last for long.

My brother Hans recalls another incident to do with the *Neurath Bunker*. In 1944 Aunt Hed (Hedwig, mother's sister), who lived in *Mülheim* on *Bach* Street, couldn't stand it there any longer. The street was particularly dangerous as it was just a few hundred metres from the *Mülheim* Bridge crossing the Rhine, which was increasingly the target of air-strikes.

So Aunt Hed took her two daughters, Betty and Leni, to live in her 'second home', the *Neurath Bunker*. Her husband, Uncle Hans, and son Lud (Ludwig) stayed behind in *Bach* Street.

On 14-15th October 1944 there was yet another attack on *Mülheim* / Cologne, during which the USAAF bomber fleet (800 planes) was able to

Mülheim suspension bridge – target of countless Anglo-American bomb raids

One of the American B 17 bombers (bottom right) bombing Mülheim bridge on 15th October 1944. At this raid the bridge was totally destroyed. Notice the impact's in the water.

come in low – the air-defences were powerless by this time. Uncle Hans and Ludwig survived the attack, sheltering in the cellar, but were half-buried. The trouble was Uncle Hans was blinded.

When the attack was over, the two of them dragged themselves to the *Neurath Bunker*. Uncle Hans took Lud's arm and the boy carried more than led his father through the flaming inferno. My brother Hans recalls: "Suddenly the *Bunker* cell door opened and there stood Uncle Hans and Lud. We stared at them for several seconds, then – despite their tragic situation and their suffering – we started roaring with laughter. The two of them looked like charcoal burners. Their clothes hung in shreds, singed and burned; their faces coal-black, but dusted with a grey powder; their singed hair, also powdered grey, stood on end in tufts; the only colour was in their lips. On top of that, Uncle Hans had his eyes closed and was carrying an old sack of family possessions on his shoulder. The 'joke' did not last long, and naturally we looked after both of them. Uncle Hans regained his sight after a few weeks."

The Mülheim attack of 14-15th October 1944 cost 543 people their lives and another 87 were never found; 2,239 apartment-houses were destroyed, leaving 8,500 homeless. The historic *Mülheim* town centre was simply blotted out. And the very fine *Mülheim* suspension-bridge, painted light green, was finally destroyed.

6

A Family-Arranged Evacuation To Silesia

The first heavy air-raid on Cologne in May 1942 brought big changes for Hans and me. Mother and Father wanted to get us boys out of the danger zone. They were working full-time, with Oma looking after us during the day. Auntie Barbara and daughter Leni were bombed out by the raid, so her husband's parents offered a temporary home. They lived in *Hindenburg*, Upper Silesia (Poland today).

In short: Hans and I were sent off with them and found ourselves in *Zaborzsche* village, which had become a suburb of *Hindenburg*,[15a] almost completely losing its country aspect in the process. It was now mainly industrial and most people earned their living in the coal-mines and the huge *Donnersmark* steel-works. Here, far to the east, all was quiet. The skies were at peace: no bombs, no bomber planes, no air-raid sirens. But there were *Flak*-batteries to protect the area.

From Cologne to Hindenburg (Zabrze, Poland today)

Hindenburg city, upper Silesia, today the Polish town Zabrze

Amongst my enduring memories is the *Schanawka*, a stream then dividing Germany and Poland, a great place to play and catch sticklebacks. Then there were the fires we lit in the fields in the Autumn to roast potatoes speared on sticks – and my first prank, which became a story to be told again and again all round the family, even years after the War: One day, on my own again and at a loose end, I wandered down to one of the *Flak*-batteries, where the servicemen happened to be on laundry and patching duty. Several of the artillerymen turned out to be genuine Cologners and, to their delight, I could swop banter with them in real Cologne-dialect. [16] Then, on some devilish impulse, or perhaps wanting to talk big or at least be their 'good friend', I told them that my Aunt Barbara would like nothing better than to do the washing for the whole *Flak*-unit. In short, a day or two later four soldiers appeared with a hand-cart piled high with military clothing and bed-linen, along with the requisites for washing them (for these were rationed). This came as a bolt from the blue for my Aunt Barbara and Leni, but they put a good face on the game and made a great job of the laundry – but just the once! I wasn't punished, only getting a well-deserved dressing-down.

But some time later Aunt Barbara pulled a far more enduring stroke on me and my brother Hans. Christmas was approaching and she wanted to give her two nephews a gift, but she had no money, and there wasn't much on offer in any case. Somehow she found out that the Catholic Church community would be surprising all the children of the parish under the age of ten with Christmas presents – wooden tractors for the boys. To appreciate this story, it must understood that Father was an atheist, so naturally he didn't have his children baptised: the two of us were out-and-out heathens. At any rate, off went Aunt Bäb to the priest and proposed an exchange: You, dear Reverend Father, will bestow on each of my nephews a wooden tractor with trailer, and I will give you two heathen-children for Roman Catholic baptism! One condition: tractors first, baptism after. Thus it was that we were baptised on the 25th January 1943 in the Franciscan Church, *Hindenburg* East, 446 *Kronprinzenstrasse*, by Fr. Josef Bennek. I was six years and four months old and it was Hans' eighth birthday! Like the rest of the Gross family from *Daun (Eifel)*, Aunt Barbara was Catholic through and through. But, like her sisters and brother, she didn't practise though believing in God. It's quite likely that she already had it in

Hans and me with cousin Leni (right) and aunt Barbara (centre) in Hindenburg upper Silesia

mind to arrange that baptism, though it was illegal to do it without parental consent: the Christmas presents simply provided the occasion.

When Father and Mother later visited Upper Silesia, Father accepted the baptism without a word, making no reproach. Later I was often to be surprised at his capacity for tolerance. Mother would have been agreeable in any case.

I'll never forget those few days when we had Father entirely to ourselves. Every day Pap took us into *Hindenburg*, where there was an indoor swimming pool, and I made my first strokes under his direction.

I had a further experience in Upper Silesia – one which made a less enduring impression – my introduction to schooling. My abiding memory right from the first day was the repulsive smell of the place which never left it. The whole school was pervaded with the bad odour of some oil used on the deal boards, which was mixed with the stink of urine and the carbolic used on the piss-channel and the wall above in the boys' toilet.

Sitting still on a school-bench was irksome, I couldn't follow what the mistress required, and the strange sounds uttered by my German fellow-pupils were intolerable – the more so because of their sarcasm about this

25

St. Francis
Church,
Hindenburg,
where I was
baptised

'foreigner' from the German heartland [17] and their constant ridiculing of the way I spoke. Consequently I developed skills for evading these daily tortures. Sometimes my toe was sprained and I could scarcely walk, then I coughed for a week, or there was some other health problem. I was to hear the word 'malingerer' for the first time from my Aunt Barbara.

When the sudden attacks of grave illness no longer did the trick, I devised another tactic: I'd leave for school nice and early, but walk past it. Sometimes I'd walk back to the *Schanawka*, where you could slide really well on the iced-up tributaries and inlets. Or I'd stroll over to the cemetery by the school, where I once witnessed the formal interment of an airman. The soldiers stood at attention along the open grave – in a line so straight it might have been drawn with a ruler – wearing air-force *(Luftwaffe)* dress-uniforms, with steel helmets and carbines, and an officer stood with drawn sabre. There was a command and the carbines jerked up, aim high, fire! Three times there was a volley; three times it sounded like one shot. Terrific, I liked that. Not though Aunt Barbara when the school authorities

Berechtigt nicht zu bevorzugtem Einkauf

Ausweis für Fliegergeschädigte

Der Inhaber dieses Ausweises

Remmel   Christian
    Name   Vorname
geb. 15.9.04.

sowie Ehefrau   Eva   geb. 20.4.06
                  Name
und 2 Kinder sowie / sonstige Angehörige,
bisherige Wohnung   Kolerweg   N. Hötrenha
sind fliegergeschädigt.
Alle Parteidienststellen und Behörden werden um weitgehende Unterstützung gebeten.
Köln, den 10. 7. 1943

                    Der Leiter der Einsatzbefehlsstelle
Unterschrift des Ausstellers: Sondereinsatz der NSDAP. Köln:

Official pass for those who have been bombed out of their homes, entitling the family to preferential help from the Nazi-authorities gave her a lecture over my truancy. After that she or Leni escorted me into school – a disgrace. School remained my enduring hate!

One day Mother and Father suddenly re-appeared, very worried, their faces serious. Our *Neurath* flat had been bombed! During the air-raid on Cologne of 8th and 9th July 1943, some stupid bombardier released his mixed load of explosive and incendiary bombs either too early or too late. Several of the explosive bombs fell somewhere else in *Höhenhaus*: the river-estate near *Wupper* Square. Ours was the only hit in *Neurath*: two or three incendiaries easily crashed through the roof. All the other bombs fell harmlessly on the bleaching-greens, the roads, and the paths.

Because everyone from our block was sheltering in the *Bunker*, and all the neighbours too, the fire-fighting could only start after the fire had consumed Oma and Opa's attic flat and reached our landing. The apartment had gone, along with its contents. My parents found a new home, still in *Goslar* Way, a couple of entrances along, but it was just one room. Crowding into limited accommodation was nothing unusual by then.

Father was sure that the war in the east was lost and that the ground war would soon be spreading west through Poland and the eastern border areas of Germany. So it was back to Cologne with the children.

7

Back In Cologne

Apart from having smaller quarters, things in Neurath weren't that different. The air-raid warnings were now so frequent that people had adapted. Instead of rushing off to the bunker at every alarm they'd stay at home in their cellars, even though these gave absolutely no protection against a direct hit. The local wardens, charged with chasing everyone into the Bunker, were completely over-stretched. People listened to mains radio air raid warnings, which gave the bomber flight-paths and their general direction. A radio station sent out a continuous steady warning beat. If it suddenly stopped, everyone pricked up their ears. Sounding just like traffic reports nowadays, the announcer would drily note: "Attention. Attention. Air situation report. It is 14.30 hours. Strong enemy formations in flight over ....". If the flight direction was regarded as safe, the usual remark would be: "That doesn't affect us" and we'd stay home despite the howling sirens. But it was quite otherwise if *Mönchengladbach* was mentioned, then we'd whisk off and there'd be no loungers on *Bode* Street.

Somehow or other life went on. Occasionally, Father would get a Sunday off work and he'd take us for a walk and "to make visits". Sometimes we'd go to *Mülheim*, where people had allotment-gardens right on the Rhine, and where a friend of his had made himself and his wife a home in their garden shed. Other times we'd visit a friend in *Dellbrück* or *Holweide*. What us boys didn't know then was that Father was keeping former comrades in touch with each other. But more of that later.

At any rate, the excursions were no burden to us. Pap had stories enough for the whole walk. Meanwhile Mother would have prepared our midday meal. Even today I can recall catching the smell of *Sauerbraten* [18] as we opened the front-door, horse-meat as it was. And there was the pudding made in a mould – chocolate pudding with vanilla sauce or the reverse.

Unforgettable too are the trips we made with Father and Mother to *Refrath*, near *Bergisch Gladbach*, where Father's sister (*Tante* Gret) lived. We got tram 'S' to *Mülheim* and changed to the 'G'. This had big heavy locomotive coaches, which made the journey fun. We'd get off in *Thielenbruch* and run through the forest to *Refrath*. On the way we'd always stop at the water-mill and, totally fascinated, watch the wheel turning through the seething waters. Josef (nickname Juppemann), Aunt Grete's son, who was my age, would initiate us into the secrets of his country play-haunts. The high point of these visits was going to the cafe Im *Wiesengrund* (In The Meadow), where we always had cake or delicious ice cream.

More rare, but all the more memorable for that, were the visits to Uncle Klöös *(Nikolaus)* in *Türnich*. To get there we had to cross the Rhine to Cologne, and take the tram to *Vorgebirge* – again with huge, heavy locomotives which made us feel like kings. *Türnich* impressed because of the great works associated with its lignite industry and the many electric locomotives which pulled the never-ending columns of coal-wagons. But such visits dropped off because of the air-raids.

The best fun was visiting Aunt Hedwig. She was then living in *Bachstrasse, Mülheim*, where her husband, Uncle Hans, was born. He was a real Cologner Jack [19] always seeing the funny side. He worked in the Mülheim abattoir and brought home immense quantities of fat of one kind or another, which had to be rendered. He kept the whole family clan supplied.

Cousin Betty was younger than me. We'd all go and play down on the bank of the Rhine, where there was a big Memorial to Admiral Spee. Ludwig, Betty's brother, was our idol, though of course he took no notice of us little fellows. We knew he was a great footballer and in trouble with the authorities for not joining the HJ (Hitler Youth) . We admired Lud and were truly sorry when he was drafted into an anti-aircraft battery as an assistant.

In those days the custom amongst working people was for housewives to take lunch into their menfolk if they worked locally. The food was

Workers would have their lunch, sitting on the pavement outside the Felten & Guilleaume admistration buildings (left above) on Schanze Street

carried in dinner cans *Henkelmänner* (handlemen), which were round or rectangular vessels made of metal, often enamelled, and with a handle: a portable set of stacked containers for holding hot food. Usually they were divided into three compartments to hold potatoes, vegetable, and meat with sauce. If Mother was on a late or night shift, we'd bring Pap's dinner to the *Felten & Guilleaume* Cable Works (which we called Jillejumm). That would mean a tram ride to *Von-Sparr*-Street, a walk down *Schwarzer* Way, and then across a steel bridge spanning the Works railway tracks.

When the weather was fine, hundreds of workers would sit out on the pavement outside the administration building on *Schanzen*-Street, waiting for their wives and the *Henkelmänner*. We'd wait while Father ate. It was great fun for everyone: the men teased the women, most of whom, not reticent, gave as good as they got. Jokes were told and there was silliness of all sorts. Here the Cologne dialect reined supreme in all its nuances and idioms.

I have a memory of going for a walk with our Pap along *Weidenbruch* (Willowmarsh), a narrow lane in *Höhenhaus*, then through the wood to *Dellbrück* Heath. There was a gravel-pit with a slanting hoist there, just across from where the forest path joins the narrow *Dünnwald* track. On this particular day, there were prisoners-of-war at work – Frenchmen, as I recall. When the guard went out of sight, Pap gave Hans and me some cigarettes and told us to hand them out to the prisoners, which we did. Somehow this made me realise that I should not be hostile to prisoners-of-

29

The O-line tram on which mother worked as a conductress

war or to foreign forced-labour workers. If our Pap was friendly to them, they were all right.

Occasionally we'd have a terrific adventure if Father had a Sunday free, but Mother – at that time a tramway-conductress on the O-Line to *Opladen* (Town near Cologne, today part of *Leverkusen)* – was on duty. We'd get on Mother's tram in *Mülheim* for an excursion, so to speak, to the end of the line, the *Opladener* Memorial showing a Lion. We'd watch Mother at work, mighty proud of her self-confidence. She looked really chic in her uniform and was so friendly with the passengers, with whom she swapped smart banter.

But there was one time when Mother's confidence, ebullience, and sense of justice, could have landed her in big trouble. She was on the O-Line again. Some forced-labour workers were pushed into her tram-car by a guard detail at the *Düsseldorfer* Street stop. These workers, who were mostly from Russia, lived in a camp nearby and a lorry usually brought them into work in the *Bayer* Works, *Leverkusen* (at that time the company was called *"IG Farben")*. At any rate, this time a largish group of them was travelling by tram. There were already some German passengers on board when they got on, and the incident occurred after the tram started, Mother having rung off. (In those days a signal cord ran along under the roof of the tram, which couldn't move unless the conductor rang the bell.) Suddenly she saw one of the guards hitting an east-worker with his rifle-butt. She went into a fury, screaming at the guard and ordered him off: no one was going to be beaten in her tram. At the same time she gave the cord two pulls, the emergency signal. The tram drew to a halt. The guard probably realised that there could be no messing with this enraged woman – and was possibly afraid to create a row. Urged by his colleagues, he got off and squeezed into one of the other compartments. Mother rang off and the tram moved on. She was later called in by the Director of the local depot and given a mighty dressing down. But she was never again assigned to any lines which might carry east-workers or prisoners-of-war.

8

At School In Cologne

I still had a horror of going to school – now the one in *Honschafts* street in *Höhenhaus* – which is why I hardly remember a single lesson. But Miss Oertel, our class teacher, is still with me: at the start of lessons we had to salute her, arms stiffly stretched out, with a mighty *"Heil Hitler!"*.

What I do remember vividly are the postcard likenesses of soldier heroes which we collected and swapped. These graphic drawings of war heroes, reproduced in brown tones, were really dramatic.

Rommel was swapped for Udet; Marseille, the fighter pilot in Rommel's Africa Corps, for the anonymous German *Panzer Grenadier* in heroic pose. Then there were the small grey badges produced by the *WHW* [20]: miniatures of Teuton artefacts such as shields – a small red glass stone embellishing the centre – or war axes and daggers.

Complete miniature fleets – from destroyers to U-Boats could be tacked onto a lapel or collected and swapped. All this made us experts in the *"Maggele"* (barter) for which Cologne is famed, the knack of tracking things down and getting them by swopping, a skill which often enabled us to survive in the aftermath of the War.

During lessons, instead of paying attention, we'd launch slate-dust attacks on those sitting on the bench in front. In those days we juniors

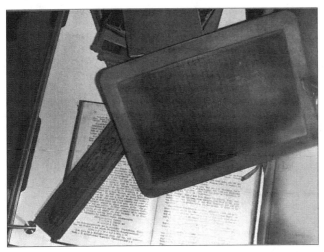

Slate board and wooden slate box for slate pencils – our learning tools

were still using slates when learning to write and we all carried our own in our satchels, protected by a sleeve. The slate had a wooden frame and was marked out with lines on one side and arithmetical squares on the other. A piece of sponge or rag, held to the frame by a cord, was used to wipe out redundant words, sentences and figures. We also had small wooden slate boxes with sliding lids for our slate-pencils and a sharpener. The slates were given points by rubbing them on a metal grater, nailed onto a small elongated piece of wood, over a semi-circular hollow.

While the lesson was going on, we'd sharpen away like mad under our desks and then would come the slate dust blast. That earned us many a crack on the head and detention from the teacher.

Right beside the school, on *Am Pfropfbusch* (At the Corkbush), there was (and is) a fairly broad bunker several stories high. Its tent-roof and tile-decking design were well suited to the estate, unlike the grey box in Neurath. Many school hours were spent there. And sometimes we didn't go to school for days on end because of the air-raid situation.

Our very military collectibles

Somehow word got around that the "Anglo-American air pirates" had it in for German children in particular and were dropping toys, as well as writing implements such as fountain pens, incorporating small explosive devices – really dangerous things. Whether this was really so or pure propaganda I've never been able to find out. At any rate, one day, probably deeply bored by a lesson, I told the mistress during break that I'd seen such a pen on the slope of the fire pond in *Neurath*. Shortly after that two senior

Germanic emblems produced by Winter Help Enterprise (WHW)

Hans (left) and Herbert

pupils in full Hitler Youth regalia came along and required me to lead them to the spot where I'd seen the devilish devices. For well over an hour we searched up and down the slope, in amongst the bushes and dog-roses, and naturally we had no luck. What with the walk there and back, a day of lessons was successfully overcome once more. There was no comeback: after all official propaganda could not be called into question.

The start of US Air Force daylight raids gave us children a thrill. Evidently the flight-path to other parts of Germany went over us, and our *Emberg Flak* was kept busy, at least in the earlier days. As other *Flak*-batteries stationed on the right side of the Rhine near Cologne were also firing, it wasn't rare for one of the high-flying US planes to be hit – and we children would celebrate with cheers. On one occasion an American bomber fell from the fleet, dropping vertically, streaming smoke, and smashed into a wood between *Dünnwald* and *Schlebusch*. Just in time the crew of the plane bailed out and we saw the white dots of the parachutes coming down from the heavens. Hans and I salvaged a yellow life-jacket from the wreckage afterwards.

One day I was out on *Bode* Street with my friends on our scooter when we heard a rushing noise above our heads. Flying extremely low with its engine stalled was a *Messerschmitt 109*, painted, strangely, in the camouflage colours of the Africa Corps. It brushed the tree tops in *Berliner* Street and disappeared behind the Zimmermann Inn at the *Weidenbruch/Berliner* Street intersection and made a forced landing in a field behind. As we children arrived, the soldiers from the *Gladbacher* Street *Flak*-battery were in the act of saving the pilot from the badly-crumpled plane. I'll never forget what I saw as I looked into the cockpit afterwards. The floor was covered in blood, and a wasp or hornet was rising from this coagulated lake, bearing away a small clot of blood. The sight of this gave me nightmares for weeks and I still think of it with horror.

We were playing on *Sandberg* when we suddenly heard a sound we'd never heard before: the howling din of engines along with dull detonations. It came from the *Leverkusen* direction. 'Our' *Emberg Flak* was silent. Looking up, we saw a strange sight. Twin-engined, dual-fuselage planes were cruising at lightning speed in a huge circle, quite unchallenged. One after the other, they'd disappear in a steep, almost stalling, dive towards the Bayer factory at *Leverkusen*, only to pull up again, resume their place in the circle and repeat the procedure.

After a few minutes they all disappeared, but banks of smoke were rising into the sky from behind the *Litze Bösch*, in the *Leverkusen* direction. This was our introduction to the American 'Lightnings': light fighter-bombers, particularly suited to low-level attacks. This was probably the first low-level attack on the Bayer Chemical Company and it had interesting consequences for us children.

Shortly afterwards we were playing in a field shed belonging to the Litz Farm, on the far side of *Flachsroster* Way opposite the farm buildings, when we noticed hectic activity on the edge of the field, just where the *Dünnwalder* Common lane joined *Flachroster* Way. In short: a small barracks went up in a matter of days, and – to our immense amazement – we saw a huge grey barrage-balloon hovering, held by a couple of cables. These barrage-balloons were to be stationed all around the Bayer Works to foil low-level attacks. After that we often invited ourselves to the army post: and sometimes the soldiers would hand us a piece of lavishly-buttered Military bread [21]. And again, not long afterwards, strange things started happening along the railway track towards *Rodderhof* (now Oder Way): barrels were being unloaded and set out at roughly 50 metre intervals. Protruding from each were (two?) thin, shortish pipes – smoke-screen barrels, supposed to protect the Bayer Works with a layer of fog.

And now we children met Soviet prisoners-of-war for the first time: they tended to the barrels under guard. At first these men seemed alien to us, even very alien, in their worn-out and shabby bits of uniform, heavy wooden shoes, shorn heads, and guttural speech. But, as we hung around and watched them work, they'd often smile at us. And, noticing that the soldiers on guard did not mind these preliminary contacts, we quickly became friends with the Russians.

One day they had planes carved from wood: big and small, one-and two-engined, with propeller, cockpit – all the paraphernalia – painted green: cleverly fashioned works of art. We held out our hands, but they snatched the planes back and said just one word, "Bread". As provision-supply was still functioning quite well at the time, there developed a barter system with a lot of the *Neurath* children joining in. "Russian planes" became something we collected. If bread was in short supply at home, we'd march off to the barrage balloon, beg for Army bread (without the butter), and cut straight back to the Russian 'aircraft fitters' at the smoke-launching station. Our barter-skills grew no end.

At some point the smoke-barrels were withdrawn. But at least we children now knew that the Russian prisoners-of-war were seriously hungry. Of course, what did we children of seven, eight, and nine years of age know of what was going on in Nazi Germany along with the War? With the end of hostilities, most of the grown-ups claimed to have seen and heard nothing untoward: "We did not know this". But even I as a

34

child knew early on that there were Concentration Camps (KZ) and that a KZ was something very bad. "Hold your tongue, or do you want to go to a KZ?" was something I heard everywhere. I also knew that this is where you ended up if you told jokes about the *Führer*, didn't observe the blackout, listened to enemy radio, blamed Göring for the air-raids, or if you changed round the words of the song, *Mülheimer Böötsche* [22] and sang: "*Heidewitzka*, the NSV [23] collects apple-peelings for the fat pig" [24].

Air-Marshal Hermann Göring was understood to be the fat pig. There were more and more substitute products, including "*Schwimmseife*" [25] a grey, feather-light, completely unscented soap – which would not lather. Rumour had it that it was made from the fat and the bones of Jews. It was also called "*Jüddeseef*" (Jew-soap). Even as a child you worried about such things, but what must adults have known?

Then even us children became conspiratorial: the password was "*Edelweiss* pirates" (*Edelweiss* = "lion's foot" a flower of the Alps). I don't know exactly when, but illegal youth groups came into being at some point: the Navajos or "*Edelweiss* pirates". This was in Cologne, particularly the *Ehrenfeld* and *Mülheim* districts. At first they were only a counter to the Hitler Youth but, after Army deserters joined them, along with escaped prisoners-of-war and forced workers, they developed into an armed resistance, notable for successful assassinations of Cologne Nazi notables, among other things.

As the *Edelweiss* Pirates were underground, living outside the system, they had to maintain themselves by breaking into provision depots. Nazi propaganda would then defame them as criminals, and they'd be hunted by the *Gestapo*, SS, and Nazi Party organisations. In November 1944 13 young *Edelweiss* Pirates were hanged publicly in Cologne and the bodies were left hanging on the gallows tree for days and days.

To us children they were wreathed in legend: no way did we see them as criminals. Sometimes, sitting around a small fire on Sandberg, we'd quietly sing the song of the *Edelweiss* Pirates: "When scouting knives flash, And Hitler Youth dash, *Edelweiss* Pirates on their heels: What more's to be had from life than that? *Edelweiss* Pirates we want to be, want to be" [26]. I have no idea how we came to have this song. Keeping mum about our sing-songs: that was a matter of honour.

9

Change Afoot

Something was up: even us children could sense it. We heard new words, mainly the names of cities of which we could make no sense: Caen, Falaise. Long before that there was Stalingrad, where something heroically awful was supposed to have happened. Now there was the 'East-Rampart' [27], the 'People's Assault' [28], the 'People's Grenadier Divisions' [29], and V-1 and V-2 Rockets. There were air-raid warnings virtually every hour and the silver fishes took over the heavens. But now we hardly ever saw any aerial combat.

An ever increasing stream of military vehicles moved up *Berliner* Street. Before, we'd only ever seen the military when infantrymen from *Hacketeuer* Barracks in *Mülheim* moved out to the rifle-ranges on *Kalk* Street on the edge of *Dellbrück* Heath. Columns of them came marching up *Berliner* Street and turned into *Weidenbruch*, us children marching alongside and lustily singing along, *A Small Flowerlet is Blooming on the Heath* [30]. It is quite possible that one of the soldiers we accompanied was the literature Nobel Prize winner-to-be, Heinrich Böll. In his *War Letters (Briefe aus dem Krieg)* he says that he was stationed in *Mülheim's Hacketeuer* Barracks and that he often used to march to the *Dünnwald* rifle range for shooting practice.

By the way: with his *Irisches Tagebuch* (Irish Diary) Heinrich Böll, having established a permanent holiday home on Achill island, made Ireland famous in Germany at the end 1950s

One evening *Berliner* Street was blocked all the way from *Mülheim* to *Dünnwald* by an endless motorised military column. The word was that they were back from France. Masses of women rushed out of the Estate to barter with the soldiers – including Mother, Auntie Bäb, and Auntie Hed. What they wanted above all was coffee-beans, which soldiers self-evidently carried in quantity. Coffee was now only obtainable on the black market and had by now become a second currency, among housewives at least. Nearly all of them carried a small metal cylinder, which often had a tiny handle: the Lot (a half-ounce measure), which was the prevailing unit of measure for coffee. But the haggled coffee-beans were still green, that is, unroasted. That was done at home. Mother had no small cast-iron coffee-roaster, dating from Oma's days, and so roasted the coffee on the hearth-plate, as did many of the other housewives. On this particular night, the Neurath Estate had the aroma of a great coffee-roastery.

10

Father Goes Missing

The sight of that retreating column and the next violent change in our lives link up in my recollection with two deeply significant turning points in our lives. On the afternoon of 26th November 1944 Father took his leave of us in the late afternoon, as was usual when he was on the night-shift. He told Mother that he would be a little late getting back as he had something to see to. But, by the morning, he still wasn't back and Mother got really worried, especially as overnight British planes had bombed Cologne. His work-mates told her that at the end of his shift he'd left the factory on his bicycle as usual. As he wasn't back by the next day, Mother went to the police to report him missing. Pap remained missing. Mother was beside herself and us children couldn't take it all in.

As Mother knew about Pap's illegal activity she got in touch with Auntie Gret who came round at once. Aunt Gret had a hunch that Pap had been 'nabbed' and she turned our home upside-down, expecting the *Gestapo* to come and search it. And in fact she did find Father's revolver in the cellar, hidden in his old coat, and she immediately made it vanish. Yet the *Gestapo* didn't come, nor was there any word from the police. Mother was in suspense, not knowing whether Pap had been arrested, which was what Auntie Gret assumed, or whether he'd been killed by the English air-raid somewhere in Cologne city centre.

In my mind this breach in our lives is bound up with the names of towns repeatedly heard on the radio. Malmedy, for instance! Nowadays we know that Malmedy was one of the departure-points for the shattered German Ardennes Offensive (Battle of the Bulge). An SS Division was to advance from Malmedy to the Marne river via Stavelot. But to us Malmedy was bound up with the call from the Nazi municipal leadership on all residents of *Höhenhaus* to get ready to be evacuated. The right bank of the Rhine was to be turned into a zone of defence, in case the American Army broke through.

Many of the locals took no notice of this instruction, while as many again did. Amongst those who did was Mother, who could not think straight since Father disappeared. But Auntie Bäb with Leni, and Uncle Hans and Auntie Hed, with their daughters Leni and Betty, also got ready for evacuation. Their son Ludwig was with the *Flak* at *Feldberg* (*Mecklenburg*, northern part of Germany) at the time.

One afternoon we found a train waiting on a stretch of the railway line near *Sandberg*. The railway-embankment was black with people, with a sound of howling and chattering teeth: after all, it was December. Helpers lifted women and small children up onto the train, for there wasn't a platform and there was a big gap between the gravel-bed and the steps of the carriages. Where was it bound for? No-one knew – to Saxony, rumour had it.

11

Evacuation To Zschornewitz

We're standing, shivering, on a platform, just beyond a great, domed railway hall. The gable-end facing us boasts a signboard: *Halle/Saale* (*Halle* a city on the *Saale* river in Lower Saxony, middle Germany). There's a railway announcement – in Saxon dialect! I'm shocked and ask Mother, "What are we doing here?". "Don't worry, boy", she replied, "everything will be alright". We're changing trains in *Halle*.

We're at *Zschornewitz*. Originally a settlement around an important power station to the north of *Bitterfeld*, it was now a considerable town. *Zschornewitz* Power Station at that time was probably the world's biggest lignite-burning electricity plant.

We're given quarters with the Grafenstein family in the colony's Power Station Estate, 1 *Neuer Weg* (New Way): just one room, but of positively feudal comfort, with a bathroom next door. Herr Grafenstein was a stalwart Nazi, but also restrained and sociable. He always wore his uniform and was the *Kommandant* of a Prison Camp outside the town – the prisoners later, after being liberated, put in a good word for him. Frau Grafenstein? Well, she certainly didn't welcome our arrival but, since we never forgot ourselves, she got on quite well with us and we with her. Aunt Bäb and Leni had a room in a house on the corner of *Haupt* Street (Main Street) and *Burgkemnitzer* Street. Auntie Hed and her family were lodged with a master baker at the other end of *Burgkemnitzer* Street, at the junction with the old *Dorfstrasse* (Village Street).

The wind blew in quite a different direction here in *Zschornewitz*, compared to *Neurath* – both at school, where there was a lot of roaring and commanding, and out on the street, where the bigger boys went around in Hitler Youth uniforms. One of them lived in our street: he had a green cord on his shoulder, showing that he was a youth platoon leader. He had his eye on us: my brother Hans hadn't joined up, not even to the *Jungvolk* [31] worse still, neither of us showed the least interest in the martial doings of the Hitler Youth.

This lad got the upper hand over us after Police Chief Apel of *Zschornewitz* nabbed us at the Prisoner-of-War Camp, lower *Burgkemnitzer* Street. We had begged Mother for a few raw potatoes for the POW-Russians and we were passing them through the wire fence. Just at the wrong moment Apel came flying out of nowhere on his motorbike and he delivered a raging harangue which left us completely stunned. On top of that he put us in the crap with the headmaster, so we got detention for a whole week.

'Us' were the brotherly duo, Hans and Herbert, along with Karli, another boy evacuated from Cologne. He was slightly small for his age and lived with his mother in quarters they'd found over the road from us in *Neuer Weg*. Karli came from central Cologne, either the *Eigelstein* or *Severin* districts of Cologne. He'd survived all the air-raids but was clearly shell-shocked – traumatised, to use modern terminology. His mouth and limbs twitched continuously and he couldn't stop fidgeting. Karli constituted our front-line verbal defensive shield against the shoulder-cord-festooned Hitler Youth boy and his youth-cohort, who never stopped ridiculing, reviling, and blackguarding us. Karli kept all the unpleasantness at bay with his rich treasury of *Kölsch-Platt* and we were his seconds. The three of us stuck together – we had no other friends, in any case.

Mother left us to our own devices. Her preoccupation was getting us enough to eat. I can't remember whether we were issued with food-ration

Zschornewitz Power Station. At the time the world biggest lignite-burning electricitiy plant.

stamps in *Zschornewitz*. If we were, they were inadequate. We were hungry all the time. Mother and the Aunts would often go off to the surrounding farmers, where food was hoarded, but I don't remember what they gave in exchange for the bread, vegetables, or potatoes they brought back. We didn't have much to offer, as we were evacuated with just three cases or small trunks.

Mother's other occupation was visiting diverse village soothsayers and fortune-tellers, who all gave her the same mysterious but happy tidings: "Frau Remmel, your husband is alive!" And, nestling in one of our cases, well wrapped up, was a pair of brown leather, ankle-high, lace-up shoes – Pap's best pair, produced pre-War at that!

Mother packed these because she was absolutely sure that Pap was still alive, would be coming back to us, and would be in need of a pair of good shoes. Despite this optimistic gesture, and despite the supernatural messages confirming his survival, we could often tell from Mother's eyes that she'd been crying, and during the night we'd often hear sobbing, weeping and whimpering.

At first we didn't notice the gradual dislocation of the Nazi-German world in general, but then it all started to happen at breakneck speed.

Neuer Way 1. The upper left window: our room. This housing estate was totally reconstructed on the occasion of EXPO-2000.

40

We would see refugees from East Prussia and Pomerania trekking through the town: they'd be sitting blankly on their farm wagons, withdrawn and absolutely silent, their household effects piled high. The only sounds were the clatter of horses' hooves and the rumbling of the steel-clad wheels. These were ghost-trek people, their faces turned to stone.

Now the air-raid warnings started up in *Zschornewitz*. During one alarm we had to crawl into a mine: an excavated lignite pit did service as a shelter. In the half-light of one meagre light-bulb we sat on benches, the inhabitants along with *Flak*-Soldiers and airmen. One of these was touched by the horde of children all round him. He produced a beautiful round tin of chocolate – Schoko-Cola, rations issued only to combat pilots, which we'd often heard about but never seen, let alone tasted – and he shared out its remaining contents amongst us children. Each of us got a piece the size of a finger-nail – a taste of Heaven under the brown earth!

Now and again we'd hear a buzzing to and fro above, at ground-level: low-flying strafer aircraft. One day we heard about a steam-roller driver, whose body was laid out in the fire-station on the corner of *Burgkemnitzer* Street (a small supermarket now). His vehicle was attacked by a strafer plane, the boiler exploded, and he was boiled alive. And it turned out to be true: the man's steamed body really was lying in the fire-station.

Then it got even hairier. One fine April day we were on our way home after roving through the nearby woods. (There was no School because the Fronts were getting so near.) No one interfered with us and we came down *Burgkemnitzer* Street on the northern edge of *Zschornewitz* quite undisturbed. But, not far from the town just past the bend, the whole ditch was full of soldiers: some dug in, others simply lying along the slope. All were in full war-paint, weapons at the ready: tank grenade-launchers, carbines, and assault guns. An agitated officer rushes out of the ditch:

"What are you doing here, are you deaf? There's a tank alarm on. Off home with you and into the cellar, but get a move on, you damned rascals!"

We didn't hang about, we were gone – but we'd only got 100 metres down the road when firing started up behind us. We dived headlong into the roadside ditch. When nothing came whistling through the air around us, no hits nearby and no explosions, we flew down the street. The *Wehrmacht* continued its busy fire in the *Burgkemnitz* direction and we did see a couple of rather small tanks circling in a distant field, but these quickly withdrew, probably because of the hostile fire.

According to my later researches, these were Combat Scouts, a reconnaissance unit of the 3th Armoured Division (1st US Army) which was equipped with M 8 Armoured Vehicles. We happened to be lucky. What might have happened if we'd been strolling down the road just a few minutes later just doesn't bear thinking about.

41

12

The Americans Arrive

Late the following afternoon, there was a whistling sound over the roofs of *Zschornewitz*, immediately followed by crash, boom, crash. US Army light artillery was firing into the town from the far bank of the *Mulde* river – seven rounds, we later heard. A shell struck an apartment block to the right of the road leading to the main gate of the power-station, blowing away the front wall of a living room.

As I now know, General Courtney Hodges ordered the leading troops of his 1st US Army (the 3th Armoured Divison – called Spearheads) to halt on the left bank of the *Mulde*. On 24th April 1945 he ordered strong patrols to reconnoitre the areas along the right bank and try to make contact with Soviet forces, which were approaching the *Elbe* river. Those were the Combat Scouts which we'd seen feeling out the Wehrmacht.

The Americans had given an ultimatum to the Power Station, which was continuing to supply an as yet unconquered *Berlin*: Either you shut down or we flatten the whole town. The seven artillery shells were to serve as a warning. The turbines were run down, but supplies for the town were maintained.

It's the afternoon of the following day, 25th April. We're sitting up in our room; Frau Grafenstein below. A scream, many screams: "Frau Remmel, Frau Remmel, the Americans are coming. They're outside the gate of my husband's camp."

Her husband had rung to say goodbye. We look at Mother: she's quite relaxed. She knew the Amis (as we nicknamed the Americans). They'd briefly occupied the *Eifel* after the Great War. Two of her sisters married Americans and were living in the USA and she'd kept up a correspondence with them up to 1941. The Amis won't do anything to us. "Mother, may we go out", we begged her. We may. So, out onto the empty street. (The Grafensteins weren't the only ones with a phone.) We whistle for our Karli to come out: "Karli, come out, the Amis are here!" He came, hyperactive as ever: "Where are they, where are they?"

First: consideration of strategy and tactics: Herr Grafenstein's Camp is to the east of the town, near the great Transformer Works in the *Burgkemnitz* direction. Therefore: that's where they must be coming from, the direction of the school and the railway station. We make straight for the Main Street (now the Street of Peace), and seat ourselves on the kerbstone

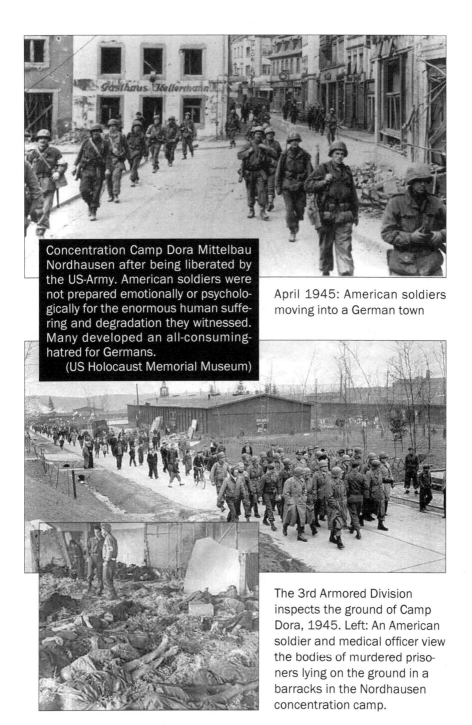

Concentration Camp Dora Mittelbau Nordhausen after being liberated by the US-Army. American soldiers were not prepared emotionally or psychologically for the enormous human suffering and degradation they witnessed. Many developed an all-consuming-hatred for Germans. (US Holocaust Memorial Museum)

April 1945: American soldiers moving into a German town

The 3rd Armored Division inspects the ground of Camp Dora, 1945. Left: An American soldier and medical officer view the bodies of murdered prisoners lying on the ground in a barracks in the Nordhausen concentration camp.

43

looking towards the railway station. The sun is shining, scarcely a person about, near enough total silence. The atmosphere's much like that in *High Noon*, the Western we later devoured.

Karli whinges: "They're not coming, they're not coming, they're hiding in the woods" [32]. Because they're shit-scared.

They are not! Up at the school, where the Main Street forks to *Burgkemnitz* and *Möhlau*, there's some movement. And in fact a vehicle is coming along the middle of the road, flanked by figures to the left and right, walking in the gutter. Slowly, very very slowly, they approach. We feel uncomfortable, and withdraw to the shelter of an electricity sub-station behind us and lie along its edge: Hans beside me; Karli clinging to me, twitching but speechless. We can't see very far up the street from here. But then we begin hearing the roar of motors and the clanking of metal: a vehicle is slowly pushing itself along – a half-track: a huge machine-gun mounted on top. To the left and right of it, soldiers are walking along in file, staying well apart and wearing funny short brownish jackets, dish-helmets, and baggy trousers tucked into leggings. And the rifle – if that's what that little thing is – is carried in the crook of their arms, swinging first one way then the other. One of them, walking in the gutter on our side of the road, looks in our direction, briefly turns round, stops one moment and goes on walking: "Kids", he probably thought. They pass us in an orderly succession.

Suddenly shots ring out from the *Burgkemnitz* Street / Main Street junction, first singly, then a clatter. Just a few moments, then silence. The GIs in front of us have squatted down, then rise and move on.

We get up as well, brave now, and go forward to the edge of the road: the Americans soldiers take no notice of us. We stare at them and are amazed. They look as though they're on an excursion: not draped with baggage like our soldiers, just a field-flask on a belt at hip level – and the belt isn't even leather. We're astonished.

A car comes flying up: a small, low, quite square, dirty-brown box – the thing didn't even have a roof or doors, though it did have a white star painted on it. The four GIs in it are bigger than their car and – it pulls up at the edge of the road, just a few metres away from us. We stare, amazed, open-mouthed: what a car – a Jeep as we're to learn. It has an unbelievably long antennae, bending from the back to the front, and the Ami in the passenger-seat is gabbling non-stop into a giant phone-receiver – and that language! Two soldiers have got out, but they don't even look at us.

It might have been five, ten, minutes that we stood by that jeep and looked, and looked, and looked. Suddenly a German soldier is standing beside the jeep – where he came from we hadn't noticed – but what a soldier: ultra-smart uniform, gold and red on his shoulders, gold and red on his collar, red around his cap. Jodhpurs with a broad red satin stripe down the side, boots polished bright – a General!? He's carrying a magnificent, light yellow, leather brief-case under his arm and addressing the Amis. They behave as though all this is more than commonplace, that this person in colourful uniform is of no interest to them; seemingly bored, they exchange some gabble with him for a while – cool, cool in modern usage. Suddenly one of them seizes the briefcase and throws it in the back of the jeep, the other grabs his arm and pushes him into the back-seat beside it; they continue gabbling with each other during all this. The jeep drives on, turns, and buzzes off in the direction it came from. We're perplexed. (We thought that all the *Wehrmacht* elements around *Zschornewitz* had withdrawn after the first tank-alert the day before. Where the General had come from – and I'm still absolutely convinced that he was a General – I have no idea. Subsequent research has brought no enlightenment about what such a senior officer was doing in *Zschornewitz*.)

Then, excited, it's home to Mother and back with her to *Burgkemnitzer* Street, this time through heavily crowded streets. The locals are now lining the pavements, gaping. Meanwhile a whole lot of US Army vehicles have parked down the side of the street. A row of German soldiers, or at least people in uniform, are standing on the far side of the road, hands folded on their heads.

Suddenly a fire-brigade appliance comes around the corner of *Burgkemnitzer* Street. It's laden with prisoners just freed from the Camp at the lower end of *Burgkemnitzer* Street. They're laughing, shouting, and waving some kind of coloured cloths. The tender stops. The liberated prisoners sitting on it jump down, talk to the Amis; the Germans all around are so much air, no insults, no threats.

But they haul out one of the prisoners on the far side of the road, the *Zschornewitz* police chief, Apel! As later emerged, it was this fanatic who shot at the advancing Americans from his district. The Amis on the half-track responded with a burst of fire, whereupon our hero surrendered. Now he finds himself in the hands of the former prisoners of war, who've a particular score to settle with this Fascist. In short: they drag him onto the radiator of the requisitioned fire engine, drive him to the open-cast mine pit and shoot him!

We're still standing at the side of the road, and half of *Zschornewitz* with us. Some of the braver townsfolk attempt to make approaches, but the GIs, icy and distant, harshly give them the brush off. These American lads had taken *Nordhausen* a couple of days before and liberated *Dora-Mittelbau* Concentration Camp (see page 43). They'd had to witness horrible conditions there. So now they're definitely sick of Germans.

Suddenly the ranks of German onlookers is thinning out: everyone is running to *Burgkemnitzer* Street – the plundering's begun. Afterwards no one knew who'd started it. But for now they're all crowding into the shops of their long-time neighbours – and the looters exit weighed down with all sorts of rubbish, but also with hoarded provisions. We're about to join in. "Don't you dare!" says Mother. Later on we did dare and got into the shop diagonally across from Auntie Bäb's. But the place is already bare, devastated. Hans finds a small spool of thread, I a packet of ATA, a household cleanser, which had been crushed underfoot and burst open. We deliver up our booty at home. Mother is bitterly disappointed by our behaviour and close to tears: "My boys looters, oh dear, oh dear, what's to become of us". But she didn't make us take back the contraband.

Auntie Bäb gives us our first English lesson that evening: she'd served as a housemaid in an American officer's home in *Daun (Eifel)* after the First World War and she spoke it quite well. "Hav ju Schokläd, plies? Häv ju Schuinggumm, plies?" [33]

The next day we run up to the nearest GI: "Hav ju Schokläd, plies?" Flashing eyes, angry glare, loud voice, hand raised: "Go to fucking hell you fucking German bastards!", or something like that, is his response. So there's nothing doing with chocolate, at least not from this American. But we take a note of the word "fucking": it seems significant, important.

But then: An Ami's standing by his jeep, two Nazi badges on his chest. Could they like this sort of thing? And haven't we seen that people living in *Neuer Weg* were 'disappearing' things into rubbish bins yesterday? So we go to look. The bins are full: Hitler-pictures, photo-enlargements of soldiers in the family, swastika flags, painted plates, engraved goblets, party insignia, even a familiar green HJ shoulder cord! And: a Mother-Cross [34]. We take it to the nearest Ami. His eyes widen, a roar of laughter: "Jäs, Jäs!" [35]. He takes a couple of strides to the jeep, rummages about, tears open a carton wrapped in oil-paper: returns with a thick, thick bar of Hershey's Chocolate in his hand, marked U.S. Field Ration D-Box. Unforgettable! Even though there's never been another bar of Hershey's Schokläd!

The Americans only stay in *Zschornewitz* for six or seven days, then they withdraw to the left banks of the *Mulde* river. By Allied agreement

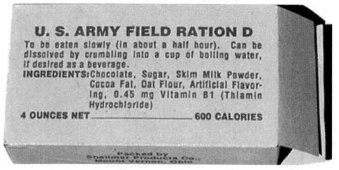

US-Army field Ration D

the river was to be the temporary demarcation line. In the town, now "No Man's Land", there's increasing disquiet: the word is that we're to be occupied by the Russians. There are several "Russians-warnings" and quite a few townsfolk hurriedly disappear with bag and baggage in the *Mulde* direction. We stay. Our young attractive female relations take on a different appearance. I particularly remember Auntie Bäb's daughter, Leni: headscarf, glasses (where on earth did she get them?), face powdered white, dark rings painted under her eyes, bosom laced flat and a small hump deformity has suddenly appeared on her back. The first time we saw her, we couldn't stop laughing. We'd no idea what this masquerade was in aid of. But Auntie Bäb soon enlightened us.

13

The Russians Are Here

This time there's no warning: but all of a sudden here they are, the "Russians". It's the morning of 4th May 1945. The first Red Army man we saw matched the cliche exactly. He came cycling up *Neuer Weg*, wobbling about on a woman's bike: his Käppi [cap] crooked and a machine pistol with its thick, round magazine slung aslant his chest. "Mother, may we?" "But be careful", says Mother.

Out on the main road the mood's almost festive, but only amongst the Soviets, it goes without saying! They sit on Panje-carts [36], playing accordions, singing: they're jolly. Again we're amazed. They've only horse-drawn wagons and a few carriages: no motor-vehicles, no heavy weapons. We see smallish units of cavalry: soldiers high on their horses, led by officers wearing round black fur caps, blue trousers with red stripes, polished boots. Slung crosswise across their chests, alongside lots of medals, are cartridges or something like that, strung on cords and swinging about: Cossacks!

Part of the column takes up quarters in the town. The big allotment garden behind Auntie Bäb's is prepared for a bivouac: all the fruit trees fall to the axe, as do the fences. A field-kitchen moves in and soon a squealing pig, requisitioned from a small-holding across the way, is slaughtered.

Was it the same day or the next? We're wandering around, our stomachs rumbling loudly: our tummies thinking our throat's been cut. Arriving at Auntie Bäb's, there's an irresistible smell of food. Just a few

47

Red Army field kitchen. Russian soldiers distributing hot food to German civilians, May 1945.

metres away down the lane, in the now fruit tree-less and fence-free allotment gardens, is the Red Army field-kitchen.

Smoke's belching from a long stove-pipe, and steam's rising from the abyss of an open cauldron, which the cook is stirring with a giant ladle – what a fragrance! We draw near the enticement, but keep our distance, staying by the corner of the house. Our mouths are watering like all the fountains of the world.

The cook, a grandpa with a giant moustache, looks over to us from time to time, scowling, very malignant. Suddenly he starts a tirade, takes the ladle out of the cauldron and viciously hurls it in our direction. The dipper misses us, hits the wall opposite and lies there. We turn to flee this raging Tartar, but immediately stop in fright. An officer is coming up the lane: fur-cap, blue trousers, dangling cartridges. He bends over, lifts the ladle, goes over to the cook: words exchange. The officer waves us over: come here! Does he really mean it? Hesitating, step by step, we approach the enticing steam. And what do you know? The cook is holding aluminium dishes, lashes a ladleful of this fragrant fare into each of them. The officer makes a gesture to us – tuck in! And, picking up spoons from a box, how we tuck in: we sit beside the field-kitchen in the grass and we spoon and blow, blow and spoon! It's thick, fatty, barley soup, with lots and lots of meat in it from yesterday's poor pig – food of the gods!

In short: after that we'd go to the field-kitchen every day at midday, armed with earthenware pots: one each for Hans, myself and Karli. And then we took care of our aunts' families as well. For the first time in long weeks we were all properly full. The cook became more and more friendly, and Mother was proud of her youngsters.

Then one day we made a really good friend: let's call him Igor. How the friendship started, I simply can't remember. At any rate, Igor was a Sergeant and a coachman! And what a coach! Aristocratic, hard rubber wheels, gleaming black, fitted out with blue velvet (but badly worn), silvery crests of arms on the doors. The thing had probably belonged to an East Prussian or Upper Pomeranian landlord. It was hitched to two great well-groomed horses: well-fed, manes plaited, harness brightly polished. Igor sat proudly on the box with his long whip. We were allowed to take turns at sitting beside him and to go everywhere with him. Igor treated us like sons. "Gans, Gerbert, Karli, come and have a drive" [37].

Sometimes it was to go and collect something, and other times it was to take something somewhere. One time we collected buckets of paint from the Power Station. They had to be brought to the forest outside the town, where the able-bodied men and women of *Zschornewitz* had been commandeered by the Soviet authorities to chop down trees. Log-houses were being put up there, the Soviets were setting themselves up to stay.

One day we're sitting in the carriage and trotting along comfortably on whispering wheels along the main street, a pleasant sound of clopping hooves in our ears. In front of us, standing at the side of the road, is our HJ enemy – now in civvies and shoulder-cord-less. "Igor, here, Hitler Youth!" "*Da, da malinki Gitler*" [38], says Igor, directs his horses a little nearer the kerb, holds the reins taut, and lays a lash on our tormentor. Aah, but that did us good!

Now we lived under Soviet rule with a curfew and nearly every day the able-bodied were put to work of one kind or another. But we Zschornewitz children at least didn't experience Soviet excesses which are so freely hawked around. Nor were these ever mentioned afterwards by our Aunts, or by the cousins with elderly trimmings (soon dropped however), or by Mother. On the contrary: we all had fond memories of Red Army men, even though we hadn't quite finished with them yet.

The 8th of May passed: the War was over. I recall no outbreaks of joy amongst Germans or Soviets. Around the beginning of June there was a council of our extended family: Mother, Aunts Bäb and Hed, Uncle Hans, our cousins Leni I, Leni II, Betty, Hans, me – along with Karli and his mother as an appendix to the clan. Unanimous decision: we won't stay here! We'll get ready to go back home to Cologne.

14

To Cologne On Foot

Homesick For Cologne is the 'national anthem' of the Cologners and singing it brings real tears to their eyes. Its refrain is:

"When I start to think of my home-town
 And see the Cathedral standing before me,
 I want to go straight home:
 I want to go on foot to Cologne." [39]

And that's just what happened!

After days of preparation, which mostly took the form of searching for a roadworthy buggy for our baggage, we were ready: On foot from *Zschornewitz* in Lower Saxonia, to Cologne on the Rhine. We had to walk because no trains were running. And in truth, but for the final 20 kilometres to Leverkusen when we did manage to get on a train, we walked every step of the way – more than 500 Kilometers!

Uncle Hans was the only one who'd managed to hunt up a proper hand-cart and, although strictly forbidden, he'd also laid his hands on a map of Germany on which we plotted our route to Cologne. To our great disappointment Mother was only able to get hold of an ancient pram, a museum-piece from the turn of the century. Unusually high off the ground, it was made of plaited straw and its spoked metal wheels were large and spindly – and they weren't set behind each other, but overlapped by a quarter. We sweated blood trying to manoeuvre it. With all our things piled up high, it threatened to tip over whenever we tried to steer it.

One day in early June we are all kitted out. Word of mouth has told us that all the Mulde bridges were destroyed and that the only way to cross the river was at Muldenstein – over a weir.

We set off and by the afternoon we find ourselves standing on the right bank of the Mulde river, but there's a bitter disappointment in store. For one thing, there are dozens if not hundreds of people with bag and baggage, waiting: all with exactly the same aim, to cross the Mulde to the West. But, in its retreat, the German Wehrmacht had blown a bit out of the middle of the weir and only a few long, narrow, makeshift planks of wood bridged the gap.

The weir on Mulde river today: We had to cross the weir over a gap bridged by wooden planks

To get across we'd have to master a balancing act. Nevertheless we'd certainly would have managed the hundred metres but for the Amis on the far bank in their Jeeps. A US Army officer – wearing steel helmet, jodhpurs, boots, short jacket – is planted in front of his men, his legs straddled and arm stretched high, holding a Colt and firing several shots in the air every time anyone approaches the weir. In a nutshell, the US Army won't let us cross.

As curfew time approaches (no German was allowed to move around in the open after 7 pm), a Red Army column marches up, officers in the lead. They halt on the river bank, opposite the Americans. The Soviet officers balance their way across the weir, negotiate with the Americans, come back, and make us understand: tomorrow, tomorrow. Meanwhile: back to Muldenstein!

We're standing on the street in *Muldenstein*, but can't get across because a Soviet column is marching through. There are countless horse-drawn wagons laden with logs and squared timber planks. Suddenly – we can't believe what we're seeing – there's a loud yell from the column: "Gans, Gerbert, Karli!" And yes, it's our friend, Igor! He's radiating joy, but – no carriage! He rushes over, hugs us, strokes our heads, embraces Mother, hugs us all. Talks and talks: *Doswidanija! Doswidanija!* See you again, see you again! But it was not to be: Igor was to remain nothing more than a lovely childhood memory of a friendly and good person.

Later on I did some research and found that he was probably an engineer in a sapper-regiment stationed in *Zschornewitz*. (It probably built the log-houses in *Zschornewitz* Forest.) This formation was moving through *Muldenstein* to a place further up the river, where they were going

51

to throw a wooden bridge across. That bridge was completed on 21st June 1945 and the locals still call it the "Russian bridge".

In *Muldenstein* we're put up in the suffocating saloon of a hostelry: hundreds of people crammed in and arguing and quarrelling. We'd noticed some semi-intact *Wehrmacht* vehicles out in the yard, including an Army *Sankra* (ambulance) fitted out with bunks. The three of us want to set up camp there and – we're allowed to. We've scarcely settled in when two young fellows come along, throw us out, and make themselves at home in 'our' *Sankra*. We're boiling with rage. As soon as it's dark we creep out of the saloon and throw two or three fist-sized stones through one of its small windows. Setting out the next morning, one of the fellows is sporting a bandage around his head: The price of evicting us! We trek back to the *Mulde*: not an American in sight. At the weir there's a long queue of people with their belongings: quick, quick, quick. Helpful hands: Red Army boy-soldiers. They get stuck in.

Aunt Bäb – dainty, but a woman of unusual determination – is for once scared. Balancing her way across unsecured and wobbling planks is definitely not her thing. *"Dawei Frau! Dawei!"* [40] Auntie Bäb is petrified with fear. In an instant one of the young Red Armyists puts his arms under her, lifts our Aunteen high and carries her on his outstretched arms over the planks and onto the other bank. Laughter all round. Then it's our turn. Uncle Hans in front, my brother Hans hanging on to the tail of his jacket, me clutching the waistband of Hans' trousers, and Karli mine. We move forward with tiptoe steps. We're on the planks, the water gurgling and foaming under our feet: I almost wet my pants. At last we're across. Mother comes across with a Red Armyist walking backward in front of her and holding her hand. Uncle Hans has already tugged his three ladies across.

And so we've reached the far bank. The Red Army boys have brought our two vehicles across: one on his own and the other carried between two. We've made it. Now a Thank You Kindly to the boys from Russia and we 're on our way.

15

500 Kilometres To Cologne

Ahead of us is a tramp of over 500 kilometres – and we aren't the only ones. We join a trail of people, with groups continually turning off to the left and right. The further West we get, the thinner the ranks. When I search my memory it always seems as though we're marching in our own bubble: my Aunts with their families and handcart; Mother, Hans, myself; and Karli with his Mother. The impressive thing about it all was that we'd no great problems over board and lodgings in towns on the way. Well before curfew we'd head straight for the former municipal offices, or for the *Burgermeister*, or for whoever was responsible. Conditions were sometimes good and sometimes bad: we were put up in inn-saloons, schools, and barns, but sometimes even in farmhouses or manors. We never had to camp in the open.

At the same time we always had to be on our guard. Former prisoners of war, along with released forced and foreign workers, were everywhere: making their way home. The Western Allies had coined the unkind term, Displaced Persons (DP) for them and truly these people weren't too pernickerty. But you also had to watch out for the Western Allied soldiers, particularly after their nightly pub-crawl. That's when they'd raise hell in the town, drunk or half-drunk, firing off their rifles or submachine gun salvos, often splintering the planks of the barn in which we were spending the night.

At first, it was that over-loaded, goddamned pram that gave us grief. The monster simply couldn't be controlled: steering it took a huge effort and it would tip over at any obstacle. Going downhill was more maddening still: instead of being able to take advantage of the momentum, all of us were hard put to it to prevent the buggy from madly racing to destruction. The torture lasted to the town of *Nordhausen* where we were sent to spend the night with families in the suburbs of this totally destroyed town. Here, with a heavy heart, Mother managed to get a handcart in exchange for Pap's good lace-up shoes – she'd guarded them like a relic till then and now she shed bitter tears over parting with them.

But it was a great vehicle for us boys. For one thing, we were able to stow the baggage so as to leave room for a cart-steerer on the front. Going downhill Hans and I would sit there in turns, the steering-shaft gripped between our legs. The other would stand behind, on the small wooden projecting base-plate, holding a strong, long pole or branch which served as a brake. For an emergency stop, we'd push the pole between the spokes of a wheel, which always worked! Huzza, what fun it was in the particularly hilly districts, like the *Harz*. And, after a particularly impetuous ride, we could stretch out on the side of the road at the bottom of the hill. Often it took half an hour and more for our group of trekkers to catch up.

It's amazing how little of this 'ramble' of five to six weeks has stayed in my recollection – and I remember next to nothing of the towns we traversed. Just particular episodes here and there have stuck through the years:

We're spending the night on a bed of straw in the saloon of an inn. Auntie Bäb had several pieces of real gold jewellery which she'd sewn into her corset, and she'd buried it under her straw bed for the night.

The next day, quite a long way on from our night's lodgings, Auntie Bäb suddenly screams out: "My jewellery, my jewellery; I've forgotten my jewellery!" Family conference. Solution: Auntie Bäb is to go back to the inn and – she's to take us three boys with her for safety. A solitary 'Mother' out on the high road alone with three children: no one's going to do anything to her. The others will go on to the next town and we'll meet up there.

We get back to the inn nearly at the same time as the next lot of 'wanderers' looking for a night's shelter. Auntie Bäb rushes over to her – Thank God, still unoccupied – 'bed', rummages around in the straw, and – triumphantly pulls out her pink corset with integrated jewellery.

We hurry back: the day's nearly over and curfew time's near. We go through a village, and can already see the

Our way home: right across Germany from east to west

village we're aiming for when we reach a cross-roads. A US jeep is parked there, and four US soldiers in it: full battle-dress, M-1s over their shoulders. A giant of a man separates himself from the group, ambles over to us, his hand raised: "Stop!" Our small, dainty, already greying – but devilishly resolute – Auntie Bäb faces this two-metre tall Hilly-Billy from Kansas, Kentucky, or wherever, defiantly. She has to tilt her head back to look at his eyes. A longish dispute flares with Auntie – speaking 'perfect' English – becoming heated, and there's increasingly threatening body language. Us three boys stand a little to the side, fearful and quiet as mice. Big American Billy points in the direction we've come from and repeatedly roars: "Go back, go back; God damned, will ye go back, will ye!" And now we're gobsmacked: our Aunteen – who weighs barely 50 kilos and is 1.6 metres tall – makes a perfect standing jump, straight up in the air, and gives Billy a hefty slap across his face, turns on the spot, turns to us three, and takes two of us by the hand: "Come boys, we're going, the blockhead can lick my arse!". We hear roars of laughter behind us. I look back: Billy is staring after us, leaning forward. The man is flummoxed. His fellow-soldiers in the jeep are splitting their sides laughing.

Dead tired, but with no further trouble, we reach the village and easily find our familiar bit of the travelling circus.

We've reached another village and the *Bürgermeister* directs us to a big farm. But Mr. and Mrs. Big-Farmer refuse to put us up. The *Bürgermeister* hasn't a clue what to do, but goes round the town. We wait; it's getting late. The community leader comes back, unsuccessful, and directs us to US headquarters adding that they don't like being bothered. A case for Auntie Bäb.

Not five minutes pass before she comes out of the command-post, escorted by an GI. Again, he's as tall as a tree, again he's in battle-dress, M-1 rifle over his shoulder. Straight back to the big farmers who'd refused us, the US Army leading the way, us ducklings in single file behind. The farm family and their farm hands are already in their feathers. The US Army of one scares them all out of their beds. Here you are: "You can sleep in them". But we don't, spending the night in the barn. In the morning the now extraordinarily friendly farmer's wife rewards us with an opulent bacon and egg breakfast.

A street winding around a largish hollow, its edges bordered with wrecked American tanks. The street's flanked with houses, damaged by gun-fire. It's early, we've already been allocated our quarters for the night and us boys are loafing around the village. In one of the gardens, right on the street, we find a German tank which looks completely undamaged: a Tiger? a Panther? We get into it, fantastic! The cannon's missing its breech and there's no ammunition, but the gun-sight and turret swivel-mechanism are working. Across the hollow, the road winds round, a plateau above it. On it small green US Aircraft are lined up: 'Grasshoppers', which do artillery observation. We get them into our cross-sights. We're playing at War, though the War itself is over!

Uncle Hans is a heavy smoker. Ever since getting to the American occupation-zone, we've a new job: picking up fag-ends. The Yankees smoke like chimneys but often throw away half-smoked cigarettes – booty for us. Uncle Hans is satisfied: he packs the half-length cigarettes into a cigarette-case. The shorter stubs are stripped of their papers and crumbled into a flat metal box. Further English lesson from Auntie Bäb: "Häv ju Zigarretts?" "Häv ju Lukki Streik?" "Go to Hell . . .!" [41]

A small woe as we're walking along! I've a raging toothache; somehow we arrive at a dentist's: "The tooth has to come out, but I've no anaesthetic", he says. "But you're a brave boy!" "No way", I say, trembling with fear. Nevertheless, out it comes. Then there was my bad, really bad, tummy-ache. We're lying in a great barn full of people. I'm bent double and writhing about. Mother's showing her Other Face, the second sight, she's praying: "Dear God, let the pain pass from my son to me". A short time later my pain goes; now Mother is bent double and writhing!

A dog has run up to us and escorts us faithfully – and voraciously – for a long, long stretch. We're at an overcrowded train-station and about to mount the only train of our long journey. Someone or other wants our dog: offers us children a bottle of wine in exchange. Uncle Hans overhears: "We won't be able to feed this overfed pug in any case – but we can drink the bottle when we get home. Despite our noisy and tearful protests the deal is done, and our trusty escort no doubt ended up in some cooking-pot.

The 20 kilometre train ride brings us to *Leverkusen* and we're in striking distance of home in *Höhenhaus*. But it's nearly curfew-time, so we have to spend the night in the *Leverkusen* multi-storey *Bunker*: Small cells, stink, stuffiness – all very familiar. In the morning, over a meagre breakfast, Mother (her second sight again) tells us about a dream she's had: Arriving in our district, we encounter the midwife who brought me into the world, standing at *Wernigeroder* Way, just past *Sandberg*. "Frau Remmel, Frau Remmel. Your husband's at home and is waiting for you!" What Mother has been wishing for!

We load up for the last stretch of our journey from *Zschornewitz* to Cologne and off we go: a few kilometres up the *Düsseldorfer* Street towards *Mülheim*, turn left on the *Stammheim* Heights into the *Dünnwald* Common lane. We quicken our pace; we're almost running – and we're singing, "I want to go on foot to Cologne". We're completely beside ourselves. We turn right into *Flachsroster* Way, past the *Litze Hoff*, past the *Sandberg*: *Neurath*!! Leaning out of an upper floor window of the flats on *Wernigeroder* Way is the midwife who delivered me: "Frau Remmel, Frau Remmel, hurry up, your Christian's at home; he's waiting for you!".

Mother's dream come true!

Pap isn't actually at home: he's expected. But all of a sudden there he is. Mother clings to Pap; Pap clings to Mother – caresses here, caresses there: kisses on mouths, cheeks, hair, and hands. We cling to Pap's coat-tails. Father strokes our heads: "Now, you two rascals, have you been good boys?"

But what does our Pap look like! What have the Nazis done to our Pap? A bag of bones is standing in front of us – emaciated to the marrow; sunken cheeks with cheekbones standing out; yellow-grey skin; eyes unnaturally large; and hair cut back to the scalp. We're seeing a fleshless skull on a very thin elongated neck, standing out of an over-large shirt-collar. Jacket, shirt and trousers flap around him like a scarecrow's clothes in the wind. That's what five months in a Nazi Prison have done to our Pap, along with the typhus fever and dysentery which caught him there.

Dad in August 1945, four months after beeing liberated from a Nazi prison

Now we got to hear Pap's story for the first time: Once War broke out, Father couldn't go on with his work of looking after the emigrants, so he enrolled in a KPD (Communist) resistance group, based on the right bank of the Rhine. At first the Communist Resistance was centralised but, after the Gestapo penetrated and destroyed it by arresting a lot of people in the late thirties, the comrades re-organised themselves into cells of three. At first these only produced and distributed leaflets, and wrote slogans on house-walls. Later they found quarters for 'illegals' – some of them comrades, but also for deserters, escaped prisoners of war, and people who'd escaped from forced labour.

In Cologne various resistance groups, along with individuals from every walk of life, came together in a kind of underground "popular's front". Ultimately, a major aim was to prevent Cologne becoming a battle-ground during the Allied advance. The plan was to have an armed uprising and neutralise the command centres of the Nazi Party and of the *Wehrmacht* in the city, thus facilitating a peaceful surrender to the Allies.

The Resistance had an arms dump in the *Deutz* District swimming baths, whose Manager was a member, though he didn't belong to any political party.

One of the people Father's group was in touch with was a Staff Sergeant of the Military Police (called the Chained Dogs = *Kettenhunde* because they wore a tin emblem on a chain around their neck) who – as I seem to recall Father's account – was based in *Hacketeuer* Barracks in *Mülheim* District and sympathised with the communists. He provided a lot of weapons – ranging right up to machine-guns, with ammunition – and these were hidden in *Deutz* Baths by Manager Heinrich Tesch, called Teschse *Fuss*, 'red-haired Tesch'. To cut a long story short: One member of Father's cell kept in touch with the Popular's Front. But the Popular's Front went up in smoke because of treachery and over 100 people were arrested by the *Gestapo* in an operation they called the "*Klettenberg* Case". The history of the anti-fascist resistance in Cologne can be looked up in official records in the City Archive under this heading.

On 26th November 1944 Father, with his friend and comrade Reinhold Hebs, had illegally arranged to meet the third person in their cell in a house in the *Lindenthal* area of Cologne. What the two of them didn't know was that the Popular Front had been penetrated and betrayed. As they entered the rendezvous, Father and Reinhold were arrested by the *Gestapo*, and they were immediately beaten up so badly that Reinhold – who had a revolver in his lunch-box – had his front teeth knocked out.

A real martyrdom ensued: they were interrogated and so badly tortured in the EL-DE House cellars, the base of the *Gestapo* in Cologne, that Father was left with permanent back problems. After that they were shifted to *Brauweiler*, seat of the *Gestapo's* 'private' prison. Then they were moved to Siegburg Penitentiary and, finally, with the Western Front approaching, they were transferred to Prison in *Butzbach* on 15th March 1945. Meanwhile the Nazi People's Court [42] passed a collective sentence of death in the *Klettenberg* Case, sacrificing countless numbers of victims. The executions in *Butzbach* were dragged out – Father believes because the prison authorities were hedging their bets – and a US Army tank broke through the Prison Gates on the afternoon of 29th April 1945. The Americans put Father in hospital because of his typhus and dysentery and, when he was better, they brought him and others back to Cologne in mid-June.

16

Life In Neurath Just After The War

Everything was in chaos in the Neurath we came back to. Evacuees were coming back and finding their homes occupied by strangers. These were Cologne or *Mülheim* families who'd been bombed out, or other homeless people, who'd moved in out of sheer necessity. We're lucky and are able to return to Pap in our home, along with Aunt Bäb and Leni.

An anti-fascist Citizens' Committee came into being and was gradually restoring order. Pap got involved with it: Social Democrats and Communists were held in respect and had authority. The important thing was that the old order had been deposed or was lying low.

On one occasion an enraged mob started taking revenge for the Nazi era. It went for one of the Nazis, NS-District Group Leader Witzel, who was made to run the gauntlet down the *Bode* Street. Everyone was thrashing him badly and the Nazi would scarcely have survived. Our Pap, himself still shaky on his feet, stepped in and prevailed. And then the Communist, not long liberated from Nazi jail, brings the top *Neurath* Nazi into his own home for protection. Pap cools Witzel's swellings and binds his wounds. A few hours later, when the street has gone quiet, he takes him home. Even before 1933 (when the Nazis took power) Pap knew Witzel as a Nazi, and Witzel in turn knew Pap as a Communist. And Pap knew that Witzel hadn't denounced anyone, hadn't harassed anyone, and had stayed fairly "decent". Besides that, in the Gestapo cellar in the Cologne EL-DE-House and in *Butzbach*, Dad had ample opportunity to learn what it's like being a victim with no rights. Here on the *Bode* Street Pap's sense of justice and toleration prevailed once more, even though he'd every reason

Neurath
housing block
reconstructed
1970

for wishing fire and brimstone on every Nazi and a rope around their necks.

Us children carried on where we'd left off in December 1944, the more so since us friends were all back together again: Tünn, Ätz, Jüppche, Querin .... now re-joined by the Remmels, Hans and Herbert. We inspected the site of the final military engagement on junction *Litze Bösch* and *Flachroster* Way. There, on the edge of the wood, was a shot-up German scout-car with two military graves beside it, complete with cross and steel-helmet. It was from here that *Wehrmacht* hold-out fanatics shot at Americans advancing along Dünnwald Common lane.

One day a demolition detail of cocky English soldiers (Cologne meanwhile had become part of the British Zone of occupation) appears and packs a mighty charge of explosives into the *Neurath Bunker*: residents are told to stay at home and open their windows. The fuse is lit! An ear-splitting crash. A huge explosive cloud. A brief groan and wobble from the Bunker and – it stays standing! It's still there today.

But what was going on in our insides made the greater impression. We were always hungry: food distribution arrangements had broken down completely. The fields belonging to the Litze and Rodder Farms were ready for harvesting, but closely guarded by the farmers' private "field-police". Nevertheless, swiping of what there was went on: ears of corn were cut; potatoes, turnips, and white cabbage were dug up. A credible story went round of how some *Neurath* boys, returning from captivity, stole one of the *Litze Buur* farm-horses one night. The tormented nag was dragged down the steps of an apartment block into the laundry room and there slaughtered with a sledgehammer. A good feed for the whole block!

At some point the occupation authorities became concerned about the starving condition of the people: they feared a hunger-revolt. One day military lorries appeared in the service area and piles of bread were handed out – beautiful, golden-yellow loaves made from maize-flour! Delighted, people gobbled it up. But the momentary joy was soon to evaporate. Half the Neurathers were struck down by the runs and sat on the toilet for hours, while the other half had cramps and couldn't go. Maize-meal does not suit German stomachs!

Honschafts Street School started up again and with it came a slight easing of our hunger. The Swedish Red Cross organised school meals: soup every day: rice or noodles, noodles or rice – nevertheless ... Added item for satchel: a soldier's mess-tin!

Then one day Swedish doctors and nurses arrive at school. Strip down to the waist, we're told, and we all have ointment smeared on a small part of our chests and this is covered with plaster. On no account are we to take off the plaster, or to wash the spot, we're ordered – it's a tuberculosis test! A week later the Swedes are back. Tear off the plasters! All of us have clear chests – all except me: mine's covered with pimples and blisters. "Look at that, Herbert has TB" (Tuberculosis), they all shout. And I'm standing all alone, the others keeping their distance. But the Doctor is grinning all over his face at the sight of me. Immune! I'm immune against TB and – a hero!

Winter was approaching and it was to be one of the most severe of the decade. Coal trains ran on a track parallel to *Honschaftstrasse*. They were brought to a halt and plundered. Or people jumped onto the moving trains and threw off as much coal as they could. This was called *"Fringsen"* in Cologne, because Cardinal Frings is said to have preached that the Dear Lord made an exception and pardoned those who stole to avoid being frozen to death. With this coming from a man of God, the people of Cologne didn't need to be told twice!

We're moving house! The Citizens' Committee has decided that former Nazis occupying spacious apartments and houses are to make room for people who have absolutely nothing and are also to give them some of their superfluous furniture and household effects. We move in with the Scherer Family on the *Pfropfbusch* estate, *Sonnenweg 20*. Herr Scherer had been in the NSDAP, a party supporter as the de-Nazification later established. He'd been an electrical engineer in the *Carlswerk* but was pensioned off early because his eyesight was failing. The Scherers occupied half of a typical two-storey house on the Estate, with a big garden. The Workers' Settlement Associations built these in the 1920s, a self-help project.

We move into the ground floor and have a kitchen/living room and a bedroom.

And we all get on well with this childless couple, even very well. Us two boys would often go up into their high attic flat and Herr Scherer would tell us about his pre-War journey-man travels all over Germany.

 Later he started coaching us, and he introduced us to the theory of electricity. And we soon made new friends in *Sonnenweg:* Aap, Heinz, Klätschoog, Jüppche, Alfred, Ätz, Robert.

School
Honschaft Street

17

Ireland?

We've survived the Winter and it's the Summer of 1946. In *Honschaft* Street School, with the holidays starting, our form-teacher is drawing up a list: "Who'll be taking school meals during the holidays? Hands Up!" Arms shoot up – me, me, me – myself among them. The boy beside me on the school bench, Herbert Wildschütz, isn't raising his arm. "Where'll you be during the holidays?", the teacher asks. "Oh", my namesake says casually, "I may be going to Ireland!" For a split second there's a deathly hush in the classroom, then a massive roar of laughing and shouting: "The twit, the twit. He wants to go to *Irrland*, to visit the erratics" (a pun: in German Ireland is pronounced *Irrland*, with double r, but an *Irrer* is a insane person: thus *Irrland* = Land of the mad).

My brother Hans has an atlas. At home we search for the Ireland we'd never heard of. Ah, here it is. An island, all green, many lakes; mountains only at the edges; small towns. Looks good, even very good. Only it's a bit far from Cologne and too near to England. In excitement we tell our parents all about it the same night. "But it's all bosh, nobody is going to Ireland", says Dad. Yet something seems to have sunk in for Father. To get one of his sons, or even both, out of our hungry life for a while – that wouldn't be so bad. Weak in chest and limb, Pap was still feeling the after-effects of his detention and couldn't work. Mother was suffering from some breast-problem and was facing a serious operation. Things were really shitty for us.

Pap must have exerted himself to find out more right away. Next day he found out where to enquire. As someone who'd been persecuted by the Nazis, Father was still in a privileged position then. He was told that one of his sons could be accepted on the list of children going to Ireland. Mother's all against it. "I won't give up my boy after all we've withstood. No! No! and No! again!" My form-teacher calls by: "Frau Remmel, let your boy go to Ireland. Don't deprive him of an opportunity he'll value for the rest of his life. The Irish are a tiny nation who are friendly to the Germans: Herbert will be well off there." Mother caved in. Thank God!

18

Operation Shamrock

This is what happened. Shortly after the end of the War, several of the European countries who'd stayed neutral (Switzerland, Sweden and Ireland) set in motion what were known as UNRRA Assistance Operations, to relieve need among civilian populations particularly hard-hit by the War. At school we'd already become acquainted with help given by the Swedish Red Cross.

In Ireland there was a particular readiness to give humanitarian help – a spontaneous feeling which was taken up by the Government. A total of twelve million pounds sterling (Euro 70 million at 2006 prices) was raised in kind (food-stuffs, medicines) and in the deployment of personnel (doctors and nurses) for the victims of the Second World War, and a lot of this went to (West) Germany. It was help from a less-developed area. Ireland – then one of the poorest countries in Europe – was the first and most generous of the countries which helped.

Along with this official help from Government there were individual initiatives. Dr. Kathleen Farrell (nee Murphy), a paediatrician, founded the Save The German Children Society which immediately got huge support. Her idea was to find Irish families willing to take in German children, particularly those who'd lost their homes and family. The Society mounted a publicity campaign around the country, which brought a great response. But unfortunately nationalistic and fascistic types also latched on. These saw the humanitarian gesture as an initiative to save German 'blood', in danger of being anglicised by the Anglo-American occupation – Ireland as a Teuton gene-bank, so to speak. Because of a vociferous agitation from this small fraction in the Save The Children Society it became discredited, and the doors to Government bodies and the Department of External Affairs were effectively closed to Dr. Kathleen Murphy and her Society. But their humanitarian concerns found a resonance.

The upshot was that the Government decided to put the whole project into the hands of the Irish Red Cross, and it brought energy and ability to all the organisational preparations, though its patience was sorely tried by obstacles put in its way. The Allied Military Control Commission for Germany, and the British High Commissioner in particular, categorically refused to authorise the exit of German children. After all, this rabble –

63

Staff member of the Irish
Red Cross with a German girl
during Operation Shamrock

children of Germans, the
progeny of the Huns, as
Churchill liked to call
Germans during the War –
would have to cross Eng-
lish territory to get to Ireland, and that was too
much for the Brits, who
were suffering from food
shortages and hard times
too. The Irish Red Cross
was forced to canvass in-
fluential personages in
public life – Church digni-
taries, Members of Parlia-
ment, Bishops, Cardinals –
to intercede. It's even said
to have approached Field-
Marshall Montgomery.

And finally they managed it: the Child Rescue Project could begin,
with the Irish Red Cross financing the costs of transportation and upkeep
of what the Irish called Operation Shamrock. But the conditions for the
project were altered: it wasn't just orphans that could go to Ireland, but
also children whose parents were in dire straits. Something like 400
children were to be brought to Ireland, but most of them just for a few
months. However some were to stay in Ireland for three years, be fostered
by host families for this period, and then they were to be brought back to
Germany. Legal problems surrounding the permanent adoption of orphans,
to enable them to stay in Ireland, were to be solved later on. Additional
conditions were that no child was to be older than ten, and 80 per cent of
those to be helped were to be Catholic and 20 per cent Protestant.

I was eligible because I wasn't ten until September 1946 and I was
also a Catholic – thanks to Auntie Bäb's bit of missionary activity in
Hindenburg a Baptismal Certificate could be produced.

19

On Course For Ireland

Finally the day arrives: probably the 24th or 25th July 1946. Early that morning we're standing on the *Neumarkt* (New Market), Cologne, in front of the temporarily patched-up Social Office – still in the same place today. There's a cluster of people, mainly mothers with their children. Flat-nosed British military lorries arrive, park at the side of the road and the English soldiers are wearing jolly multi-coloured berets. Someone in authority roars: "Say goodbye, the children have to get in". Heart-rending scenes: children hold tight to their mothers, mothers not wanting to let go of their children, crying, sobbing. The soldiers have dropped the tail-flaps of their lorries. "Get on!"

Children are lifted up, others use the metal foot-rests set into the flap and climb all the way up. Once on the flap, none of the children want to move along. Children's hands reach down, looking for mother's hand; mothers push forward, trying to catch the hand of their child. Crying, sobbing. "Please Mam, go back, please Mam, *zurück, zurück*" [back, back], the soldiers call out.

Cologne, May 1945 – only ruins left after a total of 264 Anglo-American air raids

I'm there, step onto the foot-rest, a Tommy puts his hand on my bottom and shoves: "Go on, go on!" I pull myself right up, and take one last look beyond the tarpaulin roof of the lorry. I can see Neumarkt, and beyond, past the *Schildergasse*, up the High Street, right up to the Cathedral – I could make out its main portal! My God, I think, inner-city Cologne has been bombed so flat that I can see the Cathedral entrance from *Neumarkt*. My poor old Cologne! I catch Mother's hand, Pap's hand, again and again. "Be a good boy, be careful!"

We drive, and drive, and drive. I sit right by the back-flap. Road-dust is sucked up into the truck and it grates between my teeth. It's deadly quiet on the lorry, no more crying, no sobbing; no one says a word; it's spooky.

We're in *Düsseldorf,* are unloaded at some villa: big rooms, a lot of English soldiers and German Red Cross sisters. We're told to line up by age. I'm at the front, with one of the oldest children; we've cheered up now. A nurse comes up to us, small bits of cloth in her hand, an English soldier beside her. She gets busy, pinning the bits of cloth – white-dots on a blue background – prominently to our clothes with safety-pins.

"So", she says, "you with the white and blue markers are a group; this soldier will keep an eye on you and – do what he says. Understood?" We say we have. "OK, OK", says the soldier, laughing, "OK, OK". That gives him his name: Okay.

There are ten or twelve of us urchins in the group, aged eight to ten, and we're the oldest of something like 60 children gathered here. Most of them are from *Aachen, Düren,* and the *Ruhr* – from cities which, with their suburbs, only consist of rubble. The English soldiers looking after us are obviously from the Medical Corps and they'll be demobilising at home after they've escorted the Children's Transport.

In the middle of the night – we've been sleeping any old how on tables, benches, and on the floor – we're told to get up. Back on the lorry, and we're off to the railway station. There's a train there with a *Wehrmacht* hospital-carriage hitched on, its national markings (eagle and swastika) painted over. Okay leads us onto it: we undress, get into bed, and off we go.

It's already light: we're entering a station, the train stops. There are a lot of people on the platform: mainly men probably wanting to get to work. We're somewhere in Holland, or France? Those outside most likely have found out we're German – spittle sticks to the windows, and there's hooting and shaking of fists. Okay opens the carriage door, curses like a trooper, gesticulates with his fist. The train moves on. Okay comes back, thumbs up, laughs: "OK, OK".

Again the train stops. Okay comes in to us: "Get up, get up!" Up and out: blinding sunshine, clear air, strong cool breeze, singular smell.

Looking towards the engine, there's shouts: "It's the sea, the sea!". There's a long quay, real ships – not flat barges like on the Rhine – and beyond them water, water, and still more water. None of us has seen the sea before and here it is, even if it's only the Channel. We're in Calais!

Okay comes along, this time loaded with bag and baggage. "Weit and Blu, comon!" [43]. Okay takes point, along with another heavily laden soldier in khaki; we White-Blues behind; behind us the rest of Young Germany, along with the British soldiers looking after them. But where are they taking us? We approach one of the ships. A battleship, all grey, small cannons in front, small cannons behind, small twin guns above, and a huge funnel. Hell's Bells! My heart's in my mouth: we're on a war-ship!

The sailors take charge: "Stop!" Us bigger boys, along with several of the smaller ones, are separated out: the sprats disappear through a door and are taken below deck. A sailor comes up to us: "Comon". We climb a small ladder to the Upper Deck. "Hir ju stä." [44]. Two or three more sailors: they tie some kind of vests around us. Ah, dear heart, what more can you want: Herbert's standing on the Admirals's deck – where else? If only Hans could see me now, and Pap and Mother!

Okay comes back. "Are ju okay, okay?" [45] Okay stays with us.

There's a shuddering; the funnel belches black smoke; we're moving. Hurrah! We get under way. I don't know where to look first: at the sea, a bright and gleaming deep blue-green; at the ship's prow, which is turning up creamy waves to the left and right; or at the foamy strips which the ship is pulling along behind? But still, it's all fantastic. Okay shares our joy and smiles at us. "Okay? Okay?" and he's nodding.

The vessel picks up more and more speed. There's a strong wind in our faces; it gets cold, and we start to shiver. Sometimes the bow disappears under a wave; water sweeps over the deck and under our feet: are we going to sink? "After all, we're moving on England", someone murmurs beside me. I hadn't even thought of that. [46] Another says, "soon we'll all be throwing up: there's an illness you get at sea, my big brother told me". Damn know-all! But there's no time to get sea-sick. A white strip on the horizon; into harbour: a huge, long wall with a narrow entry: we're in Dover – or was it Folkestone?

Okay is at hand: "Follo mi!" [47]. We move down from the ship and into a mighty hall with a tiled floor. There's someone standing here, looking grim; dark uniform with a lot of silver buttons and – on his head a helmet like an inverted egg-cup: a bobby, as we find out later. In the middle of the hall there's a thing like a high desk, but this one has a mini-ladder up to it, with two or three steps. Someone's sitting up at the desk and is gazing down severely from on high. Okay leads us up to it; we're in a long line. The exalted one up on the high seat looks down and hisses: "Näam?" What on earth's that – Nääm? [48]. Okay comes to the rescue: *"Name sagen!"* (Say your name). "Herbert Remmel", I say, totally intimidated. The eyes of the exalted one nearly pop out of his head, as though he's got goitre. He stares at me, swallows hard, get's up and bends down to me below and spits out venomously: "Wat dit ju sä? Rommel?" [49] Is he trying to annoy me? After all, what've I got to do with Rommel, apart from the art-postcard of his portrait in a drawer at home? Okay comes to the rescue again, looks up his list: "Not Rommel, Remmel, Sir!" The paroxysm passes off, the sick man leans back assuaged, looks down a list, makes a stroke and waves his hand: go on.

The procedure takes a long, long time: we gather by groups: Okay's disappeared, leaving his luggage in our care. Finally we seem to be moving – and Okay comes rushing up, and how! He's carrying a giant water-melon (!), clutched to his belly: and he puts it on the outstretched arms of a boy from my group – carry that! We move in the direction of the exit. Suddenly there's a dull thud. My pal's dropped the water-melon, and it's burst into dozens of pieces: a red pulpy mess on the tiled floor. Conscious of guilt, we're at a loss. The upturned eggcup comes running up and tells us off again and again: "Täk tem, täk tem!" [50]. We pick up the solid bits, the pulp stays there.

Out to the platform, onto the train. And we are dumb-founded. What carriages: the outside highly-polished dark brown, highly-polished door handles; the inside absolutely spick and span, polished wood and – all the seats upholstered with a kind a corded velvet called "Manchester" in Germany. What a contrast to our wooden-class carriages and converted cattle-trucks! What luxury! And we thought we could win a war against the likes of these!

We're in for another surprise. Okay comes along with women in uniform, young girls. They're wearing three-quarter length khaki jackets, pockets set on the outside, belt – not leather – lots of braid and silver buttons. Their skirts are calf-length and they're wearing some kind of incongruous big caps – Royal Army women auxiliaries. But how friendly they are: they beam at us and hand out small, absolutely delicious cakes, set in snow-white pasteboard cartons and with a blotch of something or other on top. And there are biscuits, filled with brightly-coloured cream: heavenly.

Okay speaks: "So long, so long, *Aufwiedersehen!*" We understand: this is a change of watch. Okay is going home and the uniformed maidens are taking over the role of caring for us. "*Tschüss* Okay!" (so long Okay). You were a great fellow!

Only what are we to do with the relics of your melon, which we couldn't get rid of and which are stowed under our seats?

The train moves off and we're glued to the windows: what a country! Lots of small cultivated fields, fat cows, hedges, hedges, and more hedges: it all looks like the grounds of a park. Houses are dotted around the countryside, no villages.

We halt at a station, scrubbed as clean as Oma's living-room, and with flowers in small hanging bowls. The platform is full of children and young people. All are wearing the same clobber and all with silly round caps. Lads of our own age with satchels! They get into the next carriage. We deride them. A scuffle starts. Our uniformed ladies have to intervene.

We're in London: the train is crawling along and halts on a bridge. We can see down through the steel struts of the bridge. There's a row of cars there, their drivers sitting in the open but the back is roofed over: London Taxis. Several of us have exactly the same idea: *Bomben auf Engelland!* [51]. Bits of melon whistle down. Whether we've hit the mark, we don't know. "But we've had a go", someone says, satisfied.

We're in the railway station – Victoria as I now know. A bus is waiting for us outside and we drive off. I'm amazed: ruins, ruins and still more ruins, just like home. We've given it to them, I think. And I believe I felt triumph. But then, for the first time – as I clearly remember – I started to ponder. None of it fits together. We give the Tommys a clobbering and they knock us out altogether. And what about Okay and our uniformed care-ladies? How nice they are to us, how friendly. They didn't need to be, after all we're the children of their enemy. It's all got beyond me.

Again we're being put up in a large villa. It has extensive gardens and it's somewhere in the middle of London. How long for? One night at least. I only remember that the uniform-ladies took us on an excursion: "Su, su, comon", which turned out to mean, we're going to the Zoo. Us White-Blues are in the lead, but we don't get far. In a Park some boys of our own age interrupt their game of football, stare at us, jabber and laugh (at us?). In a trice there's another fight and the uniform-ladies have to intervene. No more smiling now. They glare at us angrily "Back, we go back!". How come we're so aggressive? As for the Zoo, that came to nothing.

20

Céad Míl Fáilte – A Thousand Times Welcome!

At some point we repeat the ritual: bus, railway station, train, destination, bus – and we're in Liverpool Docks. There's another change of watch: now we've a couple of civilians and – nuns! The uniform-ladies have forgiven us and smile: "Good-bye!" At the pier there's a really big steam-ship – bigger even than the warship that brought us to Dover / Folkestone – the mailboat to Ireland! We're surrounded by rakish-looking passengers, mainly men.

They're all loaded up with bag and baggage, and wearing country-caps or hats. They're in great humour and sing, play the button-accordion, smoke, drink – and not just tea! These are Irish people on their way home – our countrymen-to-be!

Something like a waiting room is put at our disposal on the upper deck: wooden benches, tiny windows all round. But the youngest ones are taken below again. The steam-ship casts off, and we spend a long, long time passing through the harbour basin. Then we're on the open sea: with a strong wind, high waves: the Irish Sea is giving us a rough reception. And – now seasoned mariners – we're completely over the moon. Our nuns hover over us: they speak German.

Not an hour at sea and we're off again. Mr. Know-it-all from the Channel displays his sea-faring wisdom again: "Haven't I told you we'll all be sick, sea-sick – my big brother told me." Some rush to the railing: cream biscuits, breakfast sausages, packed lunch, caramels – it all goes overboard: Neptune's glad of the meal. Some don't make it to the railing, but are sick in the waiting-room, which now stinks to high heaven. I stick to the rail, retching again and again. If only I'd stayed in Cologne! Now I was to die all alone on a foreign ocean. The nuns comfort me.

Someone shouts: "I see land". Rubbish. I can see nothing but water. In fact, I can't see a thing: my eyes water every time I puke. Anyway, every shitty thing – it's all the same to me. Even the death which doubtless awaits me holds no horrors.

But then: a dark strip on the horizon and – two tips of buildings, Churches. Slowly, ever so slowly, things get bigger. Again there's a dark wall

Dun Laoghaire: our first step on Irish soil

70

with seaweed hanging from it, and a narrow passage, with a little light-house to the left and one to the right. White houses in the background – Dun Laoighaire, on the coast not far south of Dublin. We see a flat building, and a pier crowded with people. Long tables are laden with something we can't quite make out.

"Stop!" – the nuns hold us back to let the ordinary passengers go down the gangplank. Then it's our turn, smallest first. The people on the pier wave and wave – they're happy. They've all gathered because of us: we can't believe it. Now it's the turn of us White-Blues. Our stomachs have virtually settled, we're feeling lively again. I, at any rate, no longer want to die. We get ready to go ashore. But not a chance: one of the crew comes along dragging a long hose, and he presses it into our hands: "Big boys, clean the deck!" He indicates we've to clean the vomit out of our 'waiting-room'. We do it and play at being firemen with their pump-hose. A nun appears: "That's enough!"

Then we too are down at the tables: great jugs of cocoa, a variety of cakes, fruits we'd never seen before, thickly-buttered slices of white bread, cut into triangles and piled high. But before I can tuck in, I feel hands on my shoulders. A young couple, laughing and smiling "Jur Nääm?" [52] That I know: "Herbert Remmel". "Oh Hörbert, Hörbert, neiss Näm" [53]. I'm hugged and petted. Welcome to Ireland! The two of them talk to me and I can't understand a word. I talk to them: they understand nothing. And yet we understand each other. A bar of chocolate is pressed into my hand and then a Rosary Beads with green glass pearls (which I've still got today!) "Thank you! Thank you!" "Oh listen, he says thanks, great boy!" A piece of fruit follows – I'd only ever seen it in pictures: an orange! I take a mighty bite. The pictures hadn't told me that you peel oranges. My grimace must have been a shock to my little pair: I'm bitterly disappoin-ted. They show me how it's peeled: eat it! That I can do for myself: great, great, thanks!

The children all around me are holding Irish hands, are in Irish arms, are up on Irish shoulders. There's a babel of voices, a feeding like Jesus with the fishes. I can't take any of it in; am stunned that I'm experiencing all this: the friendly people, the many delicacies, the totally strange surroun-dings – unbelievable!

At some point we all get into green flat-nosed buses: the driver sits in front in a separate cab, the engine bonnet beside him on the outside. Upholstered seats again: we feel like Gods in France ... in Ireland. (The German proverb "Living like God in France" = *Leben wie Gott in Frankreich* is used when somebody is doing very well.) In the bus we show each other what we'd been given. My bar of chocolate is called Cadbury. US Hersheys – with their fucking German bastard – are done and dusted; now I'm a great German boy.

O'Connell Street: "I think, I've landed in paradise"

We drive through a big city: no ruins, no rubble, a lot of cars, a lot of green buses painted with colourful advertising and – with two storeys! A great broad road (as I know now, O'Connell Street, Dublin's finest road). There are thousands of lights, even though it's still daylight; hundreds of colourful advertising hoardings; and neon-lights, moving and glittering in every colour. Till now the bus had been full of the racket of children; now all – big and small – are sitting as quiet as mice. We're all staring, dumb and open-mouthed, at the motley bustle out there; at the thousand lights; at the undestroyed and undamaged houses; at the displays in the shops, which spill out onto the pavements; at the colourful, decorated shop-windows; at the many bright cars; at the many people, who are strolling, not rushing – we couldn't take it in: things like this do exist! If only Hans, if only Pap, if only Mother could see this! My God, I think, I've landed in paradise and it's not even 75 hours since I've taken leave of flattened Cologne. I simply can't take it in. Even today, when I hear or see the word, Dublin, I have that picture in my mind's eye: O'Connell Street, on the late afternoon of 27th July 1946!

21

Castlebellingham

Before leaving Dun Laoghaire we were divided into two groups. A bus took one diagonally across Ireland to Killybegs, a small harbour-town in the County of Donegal in the north of Ireland. Sticking to the east coast, our bus drove north from Dublin, a journey which seemed to take forever.

Are we in a town or a village? Low houses line a square. One of the houses is bigger than the rest: red-brick, forbidding, small gate, big gate: the Old Brewery, as I later find out. We trot in and see a yard and an elongated building. Up wooden steps to the loft: a long row of beds – our domicile; a strange smell everywhere. Not exactly inviting, I think, remembering all the overnight stops since Cologne.

Curtain dividers hang in the middle of the room, suspended from a frame: our nuns vanish in there – that's where their beds are. Later, a lot later, after someone insisted that nuns have shorn heads, we wanted to find out if that was true. One night, after everyone was in bed, we climbed up into the rafters and peeped: Aha, Aha! Our nuneens did look very singular

Castlebellingham Green with the old Brewery in the background

A young Castle-bellingham fisherman gives us a ride on his ass cart. I'm in the back row second from left.

without their head-gear. In short: these nuns belonged to the French Branch of the Sisters of Mercy, also known as Vincentians. How come there were German ladies in a French Order and why was the French Order in Ireland? That's anybody's guess.

We're in Castlebellingham, a small spot between Drogheda and Dundalk in Louth County, about half-way between Dublin and Belfast. The village is right on the coast: to be precise, on a spur of Dundalk Bay on the Irish Sea. But we didn't know that yet: that was waiting to be discovered.

The day after we arrive, hesitant and shy, we step out of the big gate, out onto the street for the first time. Immediately to the right of the gate, there's a small general store, gaily painted, little shop-window: Our noses are pressed flat against it. People go in and out of the shop, look at us with curiosity, smile – and talk and talk. They go back into the shop and come out again: "Here, some sweets!" We're provisioned with candy and toffees.

Later on, money is thrust on us again and again: "Here's a penny, buy yourself some sweets". But these Pennies are something else! Giant copper coins: just three or four of them made the pockets of our pants bulge. Once I was given a six-penny piece – though silver, it was a lot smaller than a penny. So I was that much more surprised at the mass of sweets it bought at the shop.

Discovering the world of the Irish was exciting: everything was so different to things at home. The little houses – their doors all painted different colours, knockers gleaming, huge chimneys pouring out smoke smelling

74

of turf. How astounded we were the first time we saw a donkey-cart, and how we laughed: a donkey hitched to a two-wheeled cart – we were gob-smacked!

"Farmers have invited you to have a meal with them on Sunday", the nuns told us. Cars drove up: we're invited to get in and invited to get out. My first ever ride in a car! A farm. A small cottage and a great, corrugated-iron shed, painted red and with a rounded roof; tiny whitewashed stone houses with roofs of thatched straw. Cows, pigs, sheep, a horse, a donkey. The farmer shows us round. There are three of us and we're allowed to touch the animals.

Over to the farm cottage: "Come in" is indicated to us. We're in a not very big room: we're amazed to see a big open fire-place in the gable-wall. Smoke's rising from a turf-fire and a pot-bellied iron cauldron is hanging over it on a kind of gallow. A small paraffin-lamp with a red glass shade glimmers under a big colourful picture: Jesus with an open heart! There's a dresser, with plates set on their edges behind a border and cups hanging from hooks. The table's laid – but I can't remember with what. But the Apple Pie, the apple cake eaten as a dessert: I can still taste that! There are children – two, three or four of them? They take us to the barn and we tumble in the hay, then we ramble through the little fields, bordered with mud-walls overgrown with gorse or with stone walls, and get back to the Old Brewery, dead tired and deeply satisfied.

We're given a lot of free time, aren't kept on leading strings, are scarcely supervised, are allowed to wander about and yet – despite being let run wild – are disciplined in some way that we can scarcely comprehend.

We're told we're going to form a choir. We practise – all have to participate, no exceptions – 'A Little Bird Comes Singing', 'A Hunter From Kurpfalz', 'A Cuckoo Sang On A Branch' – plenty of Hali-halo and Tra-la-la: that's a common language. We're to appear somewhere as a German Children's Choir. A bus comes for us: it's already dark – which in an Irish August means that it's very late. Was it in Drogheda or was it in Dundalk? We mount the stage in choir-formation, are beamed at by the stage-lights and by the public. Blinded, we gaze into the dark hall, see a lot of friendly faces in the front and nothing at all beyond that. But what an atmosphere! It's most likely that this was a public relations exercise and that we were an impromptu addition to the programme in a theatre or cinema? A nun steps forward, tells a story. But then, our hearts full, we sing with ardour. Was our singing terrible or was it beautiful? The public claps, whistles, rises from their seats, Standing Ovation! Was the public only being polite – or? At any rate our nuneens are satisfied, and we're being disciplined in an intangible kind of way.

The special thing about Castlebellingham was the sea, the Irish Sea: Dundalk Bay is some 15 minutes' walk from the Old Brewery. There's a long flat strand, and across the great bay there are the Cooley Mountains, with the Mournes beyond: a magnificent panorama when the sun's shining and their beauty seems palpably near. What did we know about the tides and ebb and flow? If the bay was empty of water we were as surprised as when we saw it full again. One of the times when it's gone we decide to go across the bay to the 'tangible' Cooley Mountain peninsula. Magnificent! We're marching bare-foot on the warm, slippery mud, through narrow channels with their nicely heated rillets. Stones with seaweed hanging from them; husks of some kind of sea animal; shells of many colours; bracing smell of sea. Wonder upon wonder. The rills get deeper, the water's covering our ankles, then it's over our calves. Looking out to sea from time to time, the wave-crests seem a lot nearer than before. It's only then we notice that the tide's coming in. We're not all that far from the beach: there's nothing for it but an endurance-run back. By the time we reach the shore, we're wading through water up to our hips. That was close!

We spent nearly every day on the beach: it couldn't be nicer. We liked the people in Castlebellingham: they were so friendly. The men would wink when greeting us and briefly jerk their heads to the left or right: "Nice day to-day, isn't it!" We really loved it there, despite the modest living arrangements, and despite the smell. There'd been no brewing in the Old Brewery for years: in the rooms below the loft, pigs' intestines were worked up to string tennis rackets – that was the smell!

Glencree: beautifully situated in the Wicklow mountains

76

22

Glencree

But what really stank, as far as we were concerned, was the news that we had to leave Castlebellingham and move to another abode. The Irish Red Cross had only arranged emergency accommodation in Castlebellingham because the intended reception centre wasn't ready for us. But now the new domicile in Glencree was ready for the Germans. And those who'd been sent to Killybegs joined us there.

Another bus: back across Dublin, this time going south. Then we drove through and over the Dublin Mountains, and into the Wicklow Mountains, along a narrow, sharply winding road which twisted its way through the mountain slopes. The landscape consisted of grey-brown, almost bare, expanses of never-ending turf moors which stretched far up the mountain sides, bits of broom here and there. Bare white scree patches like snow-flakes were distributed round the savage landscape: scarcely a tree, hardly a bush – just endless stretches of heather. The Wicklow Mountains are a delight to the eye when the sun is shining, but they're grim and repelling when it's misty, raining, or stormy. Nowadays, whatever the weather-conditions, they're a tourist attraction – as much for the wildness of the countryside, with the breath-taking mountain pass at Sally's Gap, as for the famous early Middle Age monastery with its round tower at Glendalough. We arrived in the rain.

Glencree consisted of three or four houses and a former British Army barracks, dating from the days when Ireland was still under Imperial thrall. The inhospitable and wild Wicklow Mountains offered a refuge to Irish patriots – who offered armed resistance to British rule and fought for the freedom and independence of their island, particularly after the French Revolution. In order to suppress the insurgents, and indeed to block them and facilitate their own troop movements, the British laid out a military road through the Wicklow Mountains. In 1806 they added the centrally-situated Glencrce Military Post: a barracks-complex made up of ugly buildings and a Garrison-Church – all built of grey granite and surrounded by a grey wall.

I must also add that Glencree is beautifully situated at the mouth of a basin-valley. In fine weather it provides a breath-taking view of the Sugar Loaf Mountain.

Also, a German war-cemetery was established here in the 1960s (why here?). The remains of all drowned German mariners – sadly drowned,

The old British barracks, our second Irish "home"

washed up on Irish coasts, and buried all round the country in the course of the two World Wars – were brought here, as were airmen from the *Luftwaffe* who crashed over neutral Ireland during the last War.

That said, near the main gate, a wild, roaring stream tumbled its way down into the valley, its waters reflecting the brown colouring of the turfmoor – and that was to be our favourite 'play-ground'. However, our abiding impression of the place was of a desert. Between Glencree and Dublin, a full 25 kilometres, there's neither house nor farm. There were no Irish people to interact with; we were totally isolated from Irish Life. From the very first minute I was 'homesick' for Castlebellingham.

There were long narrow dormitories and the refectory was in a different building. We got plenty to eat, lots of butter and there was always fresh, creamy milk. Nearly every day we got sago pudding – "frog's-spawn, frog's-spawn" would be the scary-cry around the tables! We all put on weight and rounded out: the clothes we'd worn coming began to pinch here and there.

We'd lost the nuns, but Pater Francis – a monk from wherever – took command. But the important thing was that we had Irish ladies, probably Red Cross sisters, as our loving carers. Again we got lots of free time – plenty of freedom – but also copious rain, and an exceedingly wet mist which penetrated right through to the skin – Irish Mist! I could never get properly warm in Glencree and could only think of Castlebellingham – and I wasn't the only one.

We'd made friends with each other – three boys, one with his younger brother always on his coat-tails: Conspiratorial agreements, secret planning.

78

Upstairs in the ruin in the background we had our bedrooms

We'll decamp, go back to Castlebellingham! But what's to be done with the little one, about six years old? "I'm not going without my brother", said the older boy. Well, alright. "Just hold your tongue!": we drilled that into the young lad. "Yes, yes" he swore.

Every night before bed-time we'd all have to march into Church for evening prayers and hymn-singing. The Parish Priest, who lived outside the barracks, was usually there too. Because he'd go home after the evening service, the main gate stayed open till then – our chance.

The big night came: the carers are all sitting in the front pews; we're at the very back, right in front of the entrance. We join heartily in the beautiful hymn, "O-oh Ma-a-ry help..." *(Oh, Maria hilf)*. In the middle of it we slip down off the bench, crawl back to the entrance and out – everyone here? Did anyone notice anything? No! Our nipper is hanging onto his brother's coat-tails and staring at us – he's proud as punch! We run up the road to Dublin: taking cover in the road-side ditch, we wait for a car. Here's one: a delivery-truck. We stretch out our arms, wave. And the lorry actuallly stops. To the driver: "Castlebellingham, Castlebellingham, Castlebellingham!" I can't imagine what he thought. He probably hadn't heard about Glencree and the German children there. For sure he was in a quandary. What was he to do with this strange baggage in the Wicklow Mountain desert? In short: we're allowed to get in the back and, as the front was open, we could see where we're going and talk to the driver: "Castlebellingham, Castlebellingham!" "Okay, Okay", he says, "Castlebellingham!" He drives and drives, then down a steep hill and we're at the outskirts of the city. Dublin, we're in the right direction! Not for long.

Our chauffeur halts, gets out. Oh my God, a police station! Discussion: driver/police. A policeman phones – Pater Francis? He doesn't seem to have a car available, nor do the gardai. Pater Francis has probably told them: "Tomorrow, early – after all they're in good hands with you!" We stand there, completely intimidated, shaking all over. The driver leaves, grins at us: "Goodbye, Castlebellingham!" Bastard, filthy beast! The policeman looms above us, but he isn't angry: "Germans? Not so bad. Sit down, have a cup of tea!" And that isn't all: we're fed. Policemen come, policemen go. We're introduced to the new arrivals: "Germans? Great boys, welcome". At some point they're probably getting bored: "Sing, sing German songs!" We hesitate, but then sing: A little bird comes flying ... cuckoo. Again, once more! Stock of songs exhausted. But then I remember a poem we learned in the bunker: surely the Irish would like it. I gather my courage and recite: "Chamberlain, the old swine, In a piss-pot comes down the Rhine, When to the German *Eck* he got, His old piss-pot away was shot." [54]. The policemen laugh with gusto, slap their thighs: Once more, Once more! Chamberlain, swine, piss-pot – they could understand that, and Rhine as well: that was enough. So, every time the shift changed, I had to climb up on the table and render my anti-British poem. [55] We were given blankets, slept. In the morning: Red Cross ambulance. We shake hands. So long, fine boys, great Germans!

Glencree: we get out: despondency, sadness, disgrace, ignomony, frustration, escape foiled, Castlebellingham never more to see. One by one into Pater Francis's room. He strikes me with the rope he usually wears. Raging, he beats me – on the small of my back, on my bare calves. I'm thinking, you blockhead, you bastard. Despite the pain, there's not a tear to give the Tartar the satisfaction. The little brother is the only one of us to escape maltreatment by the violent missionary clot.

Young people arrive, probably Dublin students of German. Some speak German well, others badly. Group-studies: we get a nice girl-student, go for a walk, talk to her, but then still get bored and run away, three of us. The Priest's house isn't too far from our barracks. There's a narrow yard and in it a wooden box with a tip-up lid. The box has several openings cut out of it at the bottom, so that the Pastor's hens and their chicks can slip in if a hungry hen-hawk threatens from the sky. We squeeze in, even though it's small. Our lady-student is out of her mind: her Germans have disappeared. Her fellow-students come to her aid: search operation. To get an idea of what's going on, now and again we cautiously lift the lid of the box with our heads. Observation-slit: the search-operation is still going on, good, let it! Down comes the lid. We go to peep again, heads push the lid up – crash! A mighty blow on the lid. Having discovered that we're crouching in the box, the students waited till we spied out again, then hit the lid with a cudgel. Our skulls are buzzing. The German trick has been trumped. It's one-nil to Ireland's intellectuals!

23

At The Cunninghams': Inchicore, Dublin

It's Sunday, something's going on. Cars are arriving at Glencree from Dublin and other places. People, potential adopters, want to look at the Germans, want to see anyone they might be bringing into their homes. We strut about. Look as much as you want! We're cheerful; we've been fattened up; we're high-spirited; we're well-built young Germans, all with a full set of teeth. Us you can adopt, with us you'll make a good bargain.

And, in fact, in a stone-barracks below our quarters, our carers have begun a kind of schooling, to teach us English. But the lessons are repeatedly interrupted by people who've come to pick out their German boy or German girl. We all sit at our benches expectantly: will they take me, won't they take me? Searchlight gaze from would-be adopters, coming to rest here and there. Pointing fingers "Her!" "Him!" I soon come to realise that our blond and blue-eyed Germans are disappearing like hot cakes. Unfortunately, I don't have these colours on offer: what a disappointment.

There's another knocking at the door: a young fellow walks in: tall, shock of soot-black frizzy hair. He hardly hesitates: points to me: "Him". We're introduced: Herbert, Tom. I'm excited and overjoyed. Quick as a fire-engine up into our barrack dormitory, bits and pieces packed. And I'm praying: Dear God, let Tom be a countryman, a farmer with a farmyard and cattle, fields, woods, and water. The ambulance drives up: we drive towards Dublin, then into the city, past a canal, sometimes turning left and sometimes right. This isn't going to be a farm. We drive into a housing estate. No! Not that! Suburbs, I've had enough of! But that's what it is: Bulfin Estate, 30 Anner Road, Inchicore, Dublin – the Cunningham Family.

The disappointment is soon gone: Mrs. Cunningham, whom I'll soon be calling Granny – hugs me: "Welcome!" Maureen hugs me. Olive hugs me. Tom I know by now. The three of them are Mrs. Cunningham's grown-up children. Mister Cunningham gets home in the evening: smaller than Tom, slight and thin, stoops a little when he walks, narrow face, sharply-etched features, light hair cut short: "Hello!" Then, quite late, Joesie, the oldest of the Cunningham daughters, married with her own family, calls over. She lives on the other side of the Grand Canal. The very next day she rushes off to Glencree and adopts Josef, one of my pals. So this is my Irish Family. The Cunninghams live in a small, two-storey, terrace house of the English kind: small rooms, possibly even smaller than in Neurath. This is no villa, I

1955: Granny Cunningham, Herbert, Olive, Maureen (from left)

thought to myself; if the Cunninghams have taken me in, they must be good people. And they were.

Now I'm completely alone among strangers and have to make my own way for the first time – is a particular problem in communicating as I still don't have a word of English.

After the warm welcome conveyed by gestures, sitting down by the living-room fire with a cup of tea, I'm struck by an urgent call of nature, made worse by all the excitement. Relying on my experience with the Dublin police, I speak my first complete sentence to the Cunninghams – in German: *"Ich muss mal pissen!"* Peals of laughter: the ice is broken – *pissen* is really international.

I've no great recollection of learning English, but it must have happened quickly, if not quite in a flash. Children are receptive, and the more so when the language being learnt is the only one around them. Two other German children were with foster parents in Inchicore. Hermine lived just two or three houses further along, Helmut scarcely further. I met them almost every day, along with Joesie Cunningham's adopted Josef. When we were together we spoke German — at the start. Within a few weeks we'd gone over to a mixture of German and English.

Mister Cunningham's paper — to which he was deeply devoted — was *The Irish Press*. It carried a three-box comic strip series on its last page.

At first I only looked at the pictures, but soon began to decipher the text in the bubbles.

From left: Tom, Herbert, Olive, Maureen, 1955

82

And getting Irish playmates certainly speeded up getting the language, school, less so.

Helmut and I started school very quickly, certainly within a week of me arriving at the Cunninghams. We were directed to the 'seats of honour' on the benches at the back, a great inconvenience to our class-mates, consumed with curiosity about us exotic beings. They gave themselves stiff necks by constantly craning around to look. After we'd got over our initial shyness, we'd return every backward stare with a jolly wave, or with a smart military salute – no doubt confirming all the cliches about Germans. In short, we didn't just sit – we were enthroned – on our rear bench, particularly as we didn't have anything to do because the teachers didn't really know what to do with us.

But not all our class-mates treated us as friends. The reason for that was probably that quite a few were under the influence of the English and American ham war-films, which featured practically non-stop in Dublin cinemas. These portrayed Germans either as half-savage apes, complete idiots, underhand cowards, or brutal vandals (not so far off the mark, given the 60 million killed in the war plotted by Nazi-Germany). On top of that, quite a few of my class-mates had male relations who'd fought in the British or American Armies against Nazi Germany. At any rate, we had to fight many a battle, but these tailed off, particularly after word got around about us, especially about my friend Helmut's solid boxing skills.

But once I got caught with no Helmut. One evening (probably at the beginning of Winter) I was sent out to get a family portion of Chips. The chip-shop wasn't far from Anner Road: in a former British barracks-complex which also housed problem families and was a social flash-point at the time. (The Richmond Barracks have since been demolished.) The greasy chips were poured into cones twisted out of newspaper and given a liberal dose of vinegar and a proper sprinkling of salt. Eaten without fish, incidentally, these chips were delicious.

At any rate, I'd paid for the chips and was pelting home at full speed before the chips got cold. I had to go through a gateway, past a gang of teenagers from the barracks. A war-cry rang out:" Look, the Bloody German!" and in a twinkling my bag of chips was in the gutter, with me threatened to follow. Blows rained down on me, which I could only return with kicks as my arms and hands were fully occupied protecting my head. Thoroughly thrashed, still on my feet but with the gutter imminent, suddenly my saviour appeared: an older man. He nabbed two of the louts and knocked them away, shouting abuse at them – something about "not fair!" Evidently a sportsman!

Naturally at first I was absolutely raging at these ragamuffins. After all, they'd given me a thorough thrashing, leaving me bruised and with a black eye. But I couldn't stay angry with them: the poorest of the poor lived in

Richmond Barracks (later called Keogh Barracks). I was well dressed, but these boys – and the girls too – came to school in tattered clothes and went around barefoot deep into the Autumn. Now and again curiosity led Helmut and me to explore the barracks complex and the poverty I saw shocked me to the core.

Also, I'd see boys of my age or a bit older out in all weathers, driving rickety carts laden with sacks of turf – pulled by equally rickety donkeys – loudly calling their wares. They'd be wearing country caps several sizes too big, pulled down well over their ears, along with much-patched coats or jackets generations old, usually tied around their bodies with a bit of string. Legs frozen blue.

Late in the afternoon, after the evening papers appeared, young kids would nip along O'Connell Street, a bundle of papers under their arms, putting their heart and soul into shouting the latest news. Then they'd stop, stand on some corner and blow on their blue hands to get them warm.

Beggars were to be seen everywhere and I was used to seeing people rummaging in rubbish bins.

At regular intervals an old peddler would shuffle up to the Cunningham door and open a little case holding buttons, thread, safety pins, soap and other bits and pieces. Granny Cunningham never let the old boy move on without having bought some little thing from him: "God Bless you Ma'am, may the Lord be with you!"

Even now I remember having some kind of bad conscience: I couldn't understand how the Irish could bring me and hundreds of other German children to Ireland, feed us up and outfit us, whilst quite a few of their own people — and particularly children and youngsters — were in the depths of poverty.

School again. Ours was 'Our Lady of Lourdes National School' in Tyrconnell Road, a great, granite-grey building, next to a mighty and equally grey Church and – beside a moulded concrete replica of the 'Lourdes Grotto' in which the Blessed Virgin was said to have appeared to a pious French maiden. Behind the Grotto a 'Way of the Cross' was set out and there were always people making the Stations. This is where I first came to appreciate the deep religious feeling of the Irish: this irritated me at first, but I came to understand and grow into it myself. Very soon a hobby of mine became riding about on the fine double-decker buses, the golden inscription Leyland on their radiators, especially the 24 bus. The Penny here and there this cost could always be found in the bulging pocket of my pants: the Cunninghams weren't mean. Naturally the only proper place to sit was upstairs, on one of the two front-seats. One time I had to sit behind as the front was full. But what was this? What secret orders were my fellow-passengers obeying? Almost as though on command, the men were raising their hats or caps, the women crossing themselves. Now they're doing it again – and again after a few minutes. What on earth were they doing? Careful observation revealed the secret: the hats were raised and the crossings done every time the bus passed a Church – but what about these Irish! The first few days I used to get a fright at 6 pm: that's when all the bells in Dublin, and all round the country, toll and bong up a storm – as they do to this day, even on television – the Angelus!

My second experience of formal religion was painful and embarrassing. After my belated baptism in Hindenburg, Upper Silesia, I'd no further contact with religion or the Catholic Church, let alone its practices and rituals about which I hadn't a clue.

Now my First Communion is imminent at Inchicore. Everything's ready and the Sunday when I'm to make it arrives. In happy anticipation I'm sitting upstairs in bed, waiting for the bath to become available and –

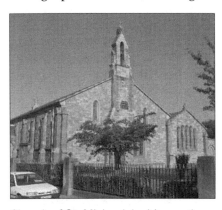

Church of St. Michael, Inchicore, there I received First Holy Communion

eating an apple. Granny Cunningham comes up to tell me the coast's clear for my morning ablutions and – freezes aghast into a pillar of salt at the door: "Herbert! Oh my God, what are you doing? You're eating?" Now all hell breaks loose. How am I supposed to know that on no account must you eat before receiving the Holy Sacrament of Communion? How come you don't know that? How come you haven't already made your First Communion? I'm bombarded with questions. But I was never stuck for a quick excuse: "Because, because, well, because the English wrecked all the German factories producing hosts!" Aghast faces, then amazement turning into indulgent understanding. Nothing was held against me. I caught up, making my Communion in the Church of St. Michael (originally the garrison Church of the Old Barracks).

We soon found playmates on the estate. Football was what we played above all, Irish (Gaelic) Football, not to be confused with the continental football, called Soccer in Ireland. In the Irish variant, a mixture of soccer and rugby, the goal posts are bean-poles as high as houses and kicking a ball through brings a point, while scoring through the goal brings three. You can pick up the ball and run, so long as you bounce it every four steps, and intersperse dropping it onto your foot and kicking it into your hands. Strong body-tackles on opposing players are permitted and the Irish love to use them.

But Irish hockey, called hurling, was paramount. It's probably the oldest team-game in the world, but it's only the Irish who play it. The wooden hurley is wrapped in a never-ending length of insulating tape to strengthen it and prevent it from snapping when striking the ball. This is as hard as concrete, and its stiff seams are on the outside. You're allowed to put it on the flat of the hurley and get running. It might be easier to say what you're not allowed to do, which is practically nothing! Fighting for the ball in the melee was like being in the Battle of the White Mountain [56]: the hurleys swung round like Dutch windmills, but everyone came out of the rough and tumble uninjured – most of the time! Unskilled in handling this Irish deadly weapon, which is said to have decimated whole Celtic tribes in ancient times, I hit one of my playmates a full blow on the shoulder: "Shitty Germans, always on the attack, what else can't yous do!"

We'd mainly play in the Phoenix Park – a massive green space 712 hectares (1,752 acres) in size – where half of Dublin sports in fine weather. To get there we'd pass Kilmainham Prison - called Goal by the Irish - which Mr. Cunningham was to tell me about. Our playing field was near the Wellington Column, a giant obelisk of light-coloured stone, commemorating the British 'sole' victor of the Battle of Waterloo. (On British reckoning, General Blücher and his Prussians played a waiter's role in this Battle – but we know better!) In the 1960s IRA men blew up a similar monument, Nelson's Pilar, in the middle of O'Connell Street: no British hero was to have a memorial in Ireland. Many, many years later, a Dublin taxi-driver pointed the Wellington Obelisk out to me: "An English hero too. But we let it stay: after all he was Irish!" (Wellington was born in Dublin.)

My second great pastime was going to the pictures. I started by going to a flea-pit (The Core) on the Tyrconnell Road, which we'd pass on the way home from school.

Soon we found out that it showed films non-stop and with no intervals from 10 o'clock in the morning till late at night – mainly Westerns. Of course

a day-ticket cost one or two Pennies, but most of the time we'd have enough. – So, after school, there was nothing to match going to the flea-pit and gazing at the films – we didn't understand much as yet, but we were persevering. The strange thing is that there was at least one film which I did comprehend, and even today I recall several of its scenes: a feature-film about the

"Our" flea-pit cinema in Tyrconnel Road   *Röhm Putsch*! [57]

The theatre cinemas in the City Centre, such as the ones on O'Connell Street, were something extra special: great palaces with comfortable, upholsered seats. First of all you could stock up with sweets and ice-cream in the brightly flood-lit foyer and you were allowed to consume them in your seat – and were even offered more to buy there. People used to smoke heavily in the cinema, as much as they liked; and my eyes popped out of my head at all the abandoned courting in the dim light. Now and then the staff would walk up and down the aisles spraying clouds of perfume out of giant spray-guns. But the absolute acme were the rainbow-coloured, irridescent, flashing *Wurlitzer* Cinema-Organs. These sat in a low pit in the stage, occupying a quarter of its width. Music was played until the film started, so you got your money's worth! The organs were arranged in a kind of horse-shoe in which the organists sat, and they were real virtuosos in those days. The sonorous sound was overwhelming. I've never since experienced music that did me so such good as those Dublin cinema-organs!

But what a fright I got when, after the film was over, a tune sounded out and a green-white-orange Tricolour fluttered on the screen: the audience jumped up as though stung by tarantulas and stood stiffly at attention. At first I thought we were getting a victory-announcement by the *Grossdeutscher Rundfunk* [58] but no: it was the martial Irish National Anthem, "We'll sing a song, a soldier's song, with cheering rousing chorus". That practice continues even now.

Maureen and Olive would sometimes bring me to these evening shows, but usually we went to the Rialto Cinema, somewhere near the Guinness Brewery I think, which also had a fantastic Theatre Organ. One night, coming out of the Rialto, we literally couldn't see our hands in front of our faces. I was never to experience thick fog like that again. Maureen and Olive were flummoxed, despite knowing the area really well. Though we stuck to the edge of the pavement, by the next cross-roads we'd lost our sense of direction. As I recall, we didn't get home till well after midnight.

Everyone in the family had bikes, except for Granny and Mr. Cunningham and usually I'd be allowed to use Olive's. On Sundays I'd go out touring with Tom: along the Grand Canal towards Milltown, or along the Liffey up to Lucan. There'd be greetings from all the cyclists and strollers en route: a wink – either the left or right eye – along with a brief nod, to the left or right, "Lovely day today, isn't it?" This all-weather turn of phrase, together with the indispensable head-gymnastic which accompanied it, was the first colloquialism that I mastered to perfection. The Grand Canal, initiated by the English during colonial times but built by the Irish, starts from Dublin and stretches through half the country. It's a rather narrow waterway, interspersed with equally narrow locks, and is traversed by narrow lighters. These were known as 12-foot (4 metre) barges or narrow boats and looked like toys – nothing like the Finow-size barges on German

A Finow-sized-barge on the Finow canal in Branden-burg

rivers and canals, which are 40.2 metres long, 4.6 metres wide and have a capacity of 170 tonnes. Brightly-painted, the Irish narrow boats resembled the gaudy tinker and "gypsy" caravans which I was to encounter later. I used to spend hours at the Inchicore Lock, with its mighty oak-beam gate which had to be opened or closed by hand, watching the family bustle on the barges.

Often Tom and I would take a bus into Dublin and stroll around the harbour. One day we saw a sailing-ship with towering masts lying along the right bank of the Liffey opposite the Customs House – it was still being used to carry freight under sail. It was unloading bricks, which were being landed by a manually-operated crane. Another time there was a news-paper report saying that the first German merchant ship since 1939 was expected in Dublin on a certain date: nothing for it but to go. I've forgotten the name of the freighter: it was still in gray war camouflage and was fly-ing the Stars and Stripes as its flag. A guard stood on the gangway, armed. Up on deck, crewmen were moving along the railing: "Hallo up there, are you Germans?" The young fellows up there are baffled: here's a Tom Thumb in short pants, standing on an Irish pier and gabbling German at them. And they were German seamen, but only the crew. The officers, and probably a few warders, were all American – and armed with pistols. "We're not allowed to do anything at all", complained the lads, "these apes won't even let us go ashore!"

Mr. Cunningham, who'd greeted me with a cool, under-stated "Hello" on the first day, and with whom I had a distanced relationship at first, turned out to be a really affectionate older gentleman with a subtle, poin-ted sense of humour – and a true Irish patriot. Indeed, as a young man, he'd taken part in the Easter Rising of 1916. About 1,500 patriots were involved, aiming to end British rule and establish an Irish Republic. The

British put down the Rising with the utmost brutality and bloodshed, using a gunboat to reduce most of Dublin city centre to rubble and ash. They executed countless numbers of rebels, mainly in Kilmainham Goal, as it's called by the Irish, the British prison in Inchicore. This gloomy, towering pile confronted me every day, as it was only a street and deep cutting away from the street where I was living.

It was Mr. Cunningham who first introduced me to Irish history, with the Easter Rising as the centre of gravity. Padraic Pearse, one of the leaders of the Rising, was probably Mr. Cunningham's favourite and he soon became my idol. Pearse was one of those shot in Kilmainham Goal, one of the 16 leaders of the rebellion that the British killed.

With Mr. Cunningham at the German Fountain (Three Nornes) Stephen's Green, Dublin, 1955

But Mr. Cunningham also told me about the Danes (synonym for the Vikings in Ireland), who founded Dublin and called their settlement "City of the cradle of the dark-water" (Gaelic: *Baile Atha Cliath or Dubh Linn* = black water) – meaning the Liffey, whose waters had taken on the colours of the many moors through which it flowed before reaching the sea at its mouth in Dublin.

He told me the story of the Battle at the Boyne River, the anniversary of which can still occasion unrest in Northern Ireland, when the Protestants, the victors at the Boyne, parade through Catholic areas with a lot of ballyhoo.

And he explained all about Cromwell, his Irish bloodbaths and massacring of whole towns. He's said to have promulgated the sentence: "To Hell or to Mayo!" – the two being interchangeable. For centuries Mayo County in the West of Ireland was viewed as the Irish poor-house and the most barren part of the island. I was soon to get to know it.

Mr. Cunningham was very fond of his pint of stout, of Guinness, so much so that it often didn't stop at one. His local was a pub down on the Tyrconnell Road, directly opposite Kilmainham Goal, and sometimes I was allowed to go with him, but I had to content myself with a lemonade. It's not that Mr. Cunningham ever got drunk in my presence, never that: But now and again he'd get a bit typsy. In the pub and on the short walk home, I learnt several Irish patriotic songs, along with some sentimental ones; and the two of us would sound these out of a silky Irish evening when we were in a good mood. It might be the Ballad of Kevin Barry, forced to die on the gallows in Mountjoy Jail (another British pile in Dublin) for Ireland's freedom; or the Ballad about the British killing all the Irish wearing green in their clothes without a moment's hesitation. But he also taught me Moonlight In Mayo, a song about the quite special light of the moon in Co. Mayo, something I soon got to see myself.

Granny Cunningham was a forthright older lady, exceptionally affectionate but also firm. She'd worked in English households in her youth, and spoke a more 'refined', and also more antiquated, English. Years later her grandsons made me aware that I'd acquired and was using some of these older expressions of hers, such as lavatory for toilet, or mantelpiece for chimney-ledge. I'll never forget the day she put on her finery, adding a hat encircled by the most beautiful fruits of the Garden of Eden, took me by the hand, and we got the 24 bus into town to get new clothes. Winter was drawing on and I only had the old German Summer things I was wearing. In the clothes shop in O'Connell Street Granny Cunningham soon got them going: she had the lady shop assistants rushing back and forth, carrying out this and that Cunningham order till I was finally perfectly turned-out. Jacket, short pants, pullover, really high knee-socks, trenchcoat and – a round school-cap with a short brim and a coat of arms, just like those worn by the English lads with whom we'd tangled on the way from Dover to London. In those days that was part of the outfit, though school uniform wasn't worn in my Inchicore School. I was really cross over this bit of headgear, which I held to be quintessentially English. I must really have been a bit of an Irish patriot.

On O'Connell Street October 1946 – on the right my friend, Josef

My first Christmas away from my family was at hand. There was no Christmas Tree: instead there was a twig of Mistletoe and an abundance of Plum Pudding. And there was a strange custom. Back at home in

90

Cologne, Mother's pride and joy was her three-winged mirror on the bedroom dressing-table: not a speck of dust was tolerated on it. Here in Ireland at Christmas time mirrors had all kinds of jolly, multi-coloured messages written on them, such as Merry Christmas, or Merry X-mas, if the mirror was on the small side. It was all colourful and joyful but absolutely not sentimental.

Although just five months had passed since arriving in Ireland, I'd got thoroughly used to Dublin: both to the Cunninghams and to the city. I moved about every bit as confidently as my Irish playmates and schoolfriends, knew Dublin nearly as well as they did, and didn't have much problem understanding what they said, though I was still recognisable as a German by my accent. And we were also taking a full part in school lessons. In short: I was well on the way to becoming a 'Dubliner'. My longing to get away from city streets and towns and into rural life, with a farm and cattle, green fields and blue lakes, was on the wane. Dublin was enough of an adventure and a thousand Irish things continued to arouse my curiosity and amazement. And, on top of that: I was well off. Things could hardly get better.

But another sea-change was in store, and once more there was a British angle to it. The War was over and communications with the colonies were again open to the British: there were no more German U-Boats lurking in the high seas. During the War Ireland helped England over hard times, supplying pigs, sides of beef, grain, potatoes, sugar beets, and the like. Now it was again marginalised and, as English demand diminished, Ireland went into recession. Whether it was great or small, I don't know. But it was big enough to put Tom Cunningham out of work, particularly as the British briefly imposed a coal embargo on Ireland at the beginning of February 1947 – which severely restricted rail traffic. Tom worked in Ireland's biggest railway repair workshop, located in Inchicore. His job finished and things got tight at the Cunninghams. Tom's missing contribution to the household budget left a hole which could not be filled. The Cunninghams could no longer do for me what they'd set out to do. They came to a painful decision: Herbert, you'll have to go back to Glencree! My heart fell into my boots: my disappointment was boundless. I felt utterly alone, was homesick and longed for Mother, for Pap, and for Hans.

24

To Hell Or To Mayo?

And yet – even in faraway County Mayo, the paper of the province, *The Connaught Telegraph*, reported that German children were in Glencree, and set out the arrangements under which they could be adopted on a temporary basis. The Nally Family, small farmers in Mayo, read this and decided to take in a German boy. The Nallys had several reasons for this: Along with Christian brotherly love and friendship for the German people, there was a measure of pragmatism – for Mae lived on the farm alone with her mother and brother and she harboured the idea of emigrating to the USA. Having a lad in the house who could make himself useful to her old mother would not go amiss. To me all three motives were equally wonderful and they were to bring about the happiest and most thrilling time of my childhood.

Just as my departure for Glencree was imminent, Mae Nally came to see her brother Joe, who was working on the buildings in Dublin, and the two of them called to the offices of the Irish Red Cross. "Oh", the people in charge told them, "of course you can make the journey up to Glencree and pick out a German. But there's one on the spot, in Inchicore, who's about to go back for such and such reasons. The lad has adjusted to Ireland and speaks English quite well. Have a look at him first." So, here are the two Mayo people, with a crying Granny Cunningham, and a Herbert torn two ways, not knowing what's to become of him.

Mae's a gorgeous-looking young woman, with rust-red crinkly hair and green eyes, and Joe's a solid-looking youth with an unmistakeable roguish twinkle in his eye. They're both farm people and know what to look out for when getting livestock. You look at horses' teeth and cows' udders – but me? They look me over carefully, the criteria being first physical, then ethnic – or perhaps it was the other way about: I'm the first living German either of them has seen. Of course, they could see my teeth, which showed when I laughed, and everything else must have been satisfactory.

"We'll take him home to Mayo", says Mae, and I can hardly believe my ears. Did I hear that right: Mayo? No, no, not me! Am I being punished? To Hell or To Mayo is still sounding in my ears, and I'm to go there? It's curtains for me. The day after next, it's goodbye to the Cunninghams – everything's very sad. "Herbert, don't forget us, you're part of the family." And I haven't forgotten them. I'm in touch with the Cunninghams, right up to present – with their grand-children now!

25

Welcome To Mayo, Welcome To Nally Farm

Mae and Joe were waiting outside in Joe's car, a version of the German pre-War Ford *Eifel*. Joe brought us to Westland Row Railway Station, which is where trains to the West coast went from in those days. We shared the carriage with others, all of them young women and girls. I was introduced. "German Boy" – What? How come? Why? from Where? From Cologne. "Oh Cologne, great city: Cologne Cathedral, Cologne four-seven-eleven." "Yes, yes: the Cathedral is still standing, the rest's all *kaputt*. 4711 is gone, everything's *kaputt*" (*kaputt* = smashed). "Oh, isn't it a shame!" Then more important things were chattered about: like the New Look; and nylon stockings, just invented and launched in the market as the ultimate fashion. I was forced to listen to all this, even though I was in a fever of anticipation for "our" stop – which finally came after three hours: Claremorris. Pitch-black February evening; a short walk through the town, which looks completely dead. We arrive at the house of Mae's friend: a Band Leader who conducts a dance-band and has a car. "This'll be your German?" he said to Mae, and he then turns to me: "Welcome to Mayo! You'll like it here: it's the best part of Ireland." I didn't believe a word of it. To Hell or to Mayo had taken a deep hold of me.

Off we go, along a tar road for several kilometres: then we turn right. In the headlights I see a country lane, narrow, untarred, a grass strip running up the middle of it. We go downhill and then steeply uphill and then turn right again. A still narrower lane: the car just fits: the headlights show earth ditches, overgrown with thorny furze, familiar to me from Castlebellingham. We drive through the middle of a farm yard: stalls to the left, dung-heap to the right. Another 100 metres and we halt. In the headlights to the left I can see the front of a white-washed house; straight ahead the gable-end of a smaller one with a huge door. I get out: There's a smell of horse-dung, cow-manure, pig-sty, and of turf-fire. God in heaven! I'm in a farm-yard: my dearest wish-dream has come true. I can't take it in – want to shout, to roar. I'm standing there as full of voltage as an electricity line. I'm over the moon.

I hadn't noticed the small house a little to the side: we go over to it. You can hardly see its silhouette on the horizon, which gives it a sinister appearance: just one window sheds a weak light. We go in. Again it's the smells I register first. Indeed, I think no other country besides the Ireland

The Nally farmhouse, photo taken 1994 after it was abandoned. Once the old house was at the left and the barn with the pony trap straight ahead.

of my childhood can be identified so distinctly by its smells. Now I can smell turf-fire, paraffin, and milk.

There's a small fire in the hearth, and in front of it is sitting an old lady, dressed all in black, combing her hip-length, silver-grey hair, my future Nally Granny. Mae introduces me: "Hello Mom, that's Herbert". Granny speaks very softly, but quite clearly, her voice very tender: "God bless you, Herbert, welcome to our house". A dog's lying in front of the open fire: he gets up, stretches, and startes snuffling at my legs. Major was a young collie, and we were to become inseparable. I look around. The fireplace, the open hearth, dominates the room: it heats the place and the cooking's done on it. Set into it is an iron gallow, from which a bulging, three-legged, cast-iron pot gets hung. To the left of the fireplace a door leads to Mae and Granny's bedroom. To the right of the fireplace there's a narrow built-in cupboard. Granny's armchair – the only one in the house – stands between it and the hearth.

In the wall facing the fireplace, to the right, a door leads into sitting room. (While I was there, it was used only for visitors from America, and that was just twice.) It has a cupboard and a table with four chairs, all made of a beautiful stained black wood. It also has the only wooden floor in the house, covered with a carpet.

To the left a door leads to a pantry, where the washing is done as well. Another door beside it leads to a small extension, which serves as a bedroom. The big living-room in which we're now sitting, with its hearth and simple concrete floor, is arranged in much the same way as I'd already got to know amongst the Castlebellingham farmers: There's a cupboard, on which plates of all sizes are held behind a border, and with cups and pots hanging from hooks. Facing it, under the window, there's a table, with

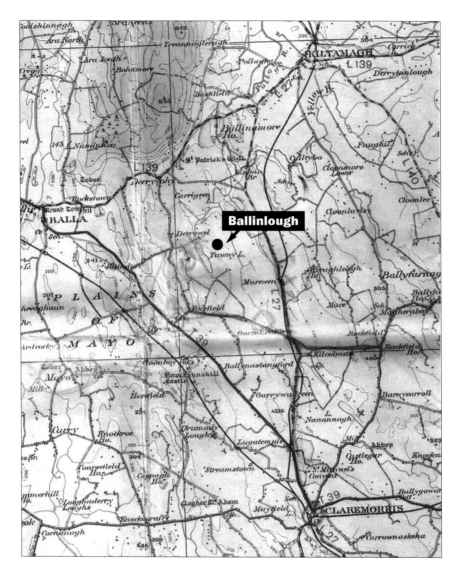

Ballinlough

three chairs. Over it is the perpetual light, a small paraffin-lamp with a red glass shade, under the usual picture of Jesus. Above us is the low, dark, grooved-plank ceiling. And now I first become aware of the paraffin lamp hanging from the ceiling, which is giving us light. It's a fact, there's no electricity here!

The area of the house was something like 100 square metres. It was roofed with slabs of slate and was typical of the standard house, built all around the country at the turn of the twentieth century, and which can still

 Eugene

 Mae.

Notice the turf reek in the background.

be seen all over Ireland. The walls of these houses had just a small proportion of cement binding the rough stone chips – which were got by crushing stones from the fields. Little was spent on render: cement was expensive.

Meanwhile Granny's been heating milk, pours it into a mug, breaks some bread into it, puts a knob of butter on it and reaches it to me. "Take as much sugar as you want." Of course I'd already got to know porridge at the Cunninghams – oatmeal cooked in water, with cold milk poured over it and sprinkled with sugar. The mish-mash now being handed to me is something new and I feel doubtful about it. Nevertheless sops (softened bits of bread) turns out to be so delicious that it became my usual bed-time snack.

The back of the Nally farmhous (now abandened). My temporary bedroom was in the extension.

The remains of our shed open to the heavens (left). Straight ahead the door of the cows-stall, 1994.

I'm in the middle of answering every possible sort of question, and of describing my Cologne family in all its branches, when we hear footsteps approaching. The front door opens and in the doorway stands a tall young man, enveloped in an olive-green military greatcoat. With a swing he sails his hat across the room. Eugene! He certainly doesn't wait for Mae to introduce us. He comes across to me, grabs me under my arms, raises me up and looks me in the eyes. "One thing I can tell you, my lad, we're going to get on well." And we did. Eugene, aged 23 or 24 at the time, was my close friend, my big brother, my great role-model. We fitted together like two left slippers. I recall us once going into a pub in neighbouring Balla after a successful bit of business in the cattle market. One of the men sitting at the bar called out: "Here they come, the United Irishmen!" Now the Nally Family, along with one German immigrant fill-in, was all together: Granny, with daughter Mae, son Eugene, and Herbert the German.

But this was the mini-version. Granny Nally had borne 13 children: all except Eugene and Mae had left home. Patrick, called Simon, was married at Murneen, not far from our farm. Likewise Martin, just a few kilometres further on, in Belcarra. Tom and Joe worked on the buildings in Dublin. Sister Patrick was a nun in England – and all the rest had emigrated to America.

As for myself, I'd landed up where I always wanted to be: in the countryside. However, that I'd ended up among the Nallys in Ballinlough, Balla, County Mayo: that was down to the lucky star I'd been under ever since Father and Mother said OK to my 'emigration' to Ireland.

26

My Irish Farm

Early next morning Eugene enlightened me as to the level of civilisation in my new home when I asked him where the lavatory was. "Well, Herbert, now in Wintertime, you can if you like go into the cow-shed for your big business. But you can also go behind the ditch, behind the hedge – our Summer toilet – which also works in the Winter."

After I'd gone away and done my little bit of business, I wanted to have my morning wash and went looking for the tap. "Well, Herbert, you have to fill this water-basin from this jug of spring-water. But then you have to see that the jug is refilled, so you have to go to the well. I'll show you the way. But you can also get water for washing from the rain-water concrete tank at the gable: that'll refill itself." After the cold weather was past I preferred to make my – not always very thorough – ablutions out at the rain-tank in all weather conditions, good or bad. I only mention this because this toughening up meant that I never had a single cold during all my time in Ireland. In 1947 Co. Mayo wasn't the only country area to have no electricity or running water, and usually no toilets (I didn't even see a plop-toilet). And - I liked that!

After breakfast – Eugene disappeared on his bike after milking – Mae offered to show me round. The white-washed house I'd seen in the car headlights the night before turned out to be the Old House – a low building, built with field-stones, where the Nallys lived before their present home was built. What used to be the living room was now where the food for the animals was got ready: the mighty, well-blackened fireplace had the by now familiar gallows from which hung a cast-iron pot – I'd never seen one as big – used to boil the potatoes for the pigs. In one corner narrow, half-size concrete walls formed a small enclosure in which the milk-calves were kept. A half-door led into the yard. The biggest feature here was a dung-pit, surrounded on three sides by low concrete walls. At right angles to the Old House was a stable-building: the cow-stall.

In it were standing the old cow (Irish farmers don't usually give names to their horned animals), a younger cow, a pregnant heifer, and – a donkey, likewise nameless – and also ball-less. I was to find out that he was a stubborn and self-willed bastard, and at first he'd have me in a permanent state of white rage. In the angle between this stall and the Old House, its former bed-room, now set up as a pig-sty, a sow was grunting with her

Bonhams (pronounced bonov). There was another stable at the other end of the Old House with six bullocks tied up in it: three to the left and three to the right.

The small house with the big gate in it turned out to be the barn. The first third of this was a 'coachhouse' for a pretty little pony-trap: with no pony, I could only hitch up the donkey to it on Sundays, when I drove Granny to Church. The rear two-thirds was a window-less horse-box. It was so narrow that the nag could only exit backwards. The horse was a strong gelding, well-supplied with fodder, called Charlie (horses do have names in Ireland) – and he was to afford me a lot of pleasure.

There still remained the hen-house, squeezed in between the Old House and the shed, which was sideways-on to the cow-shed in the garden: its framework was made of old railway track and its walls and roof were of galvanized iron sheets. Because this was used to roof all these buildings, they were called Galvanised Sheds. These must have popped up like mushrooms all around Ireland in the 1920s and 1930s. They were – and remain – all over the countryside.

The turf-reek must definitely be mentioned as well. Opposite the farm-house, on the far side of the lane, sods were ingeniously 'laid' into a longish pyramid, which provided for heating in the Winter and cooking in the Summer. The days I spent on the peat-bog, where the turf was cut and stacked, were amongst my happiest in Ireland.

The Nallys had about 20 acres (around 8 hectares): the strip-fields stretched up to the farm-house and back from it, and resemble the small-holdings in *Mecklenburg*.

A bit of bog land – cut-away bog – about a kilometre away, was also part of it. And further still were about 6 acres of rented land, called "Black Jack's". The Farm of an Irish small farmer is something like a *Mecklenburg* croft (*Buedner*). Every farmer lives on his own soil. The farms are strung out, like a pearl necklace – but at uneven intervals – along the roads, the smallest of which are called *boreens*. A settlement of this kind, sticking more or less together, is called a village. My village was Ballinlough (Gaelic: *Baile an Locha* – settlement on the lake). Balla also forms part of the postal address. It's a small town nearby, and it forms a triangle with the towneens further away: Claremorris and Kiltimagh. Our village was in the middle of the triangle.

All this was to form my realm – my farm! Stupendous, simply great. I just couldn't take it in: I was overwhelmed. To hell with "To Hell or to Mayo"! Mayo is my paradise!

27

My friend Jack

It was cold at the time, unusually cold for Ireland, which was why the cattle, the horse, and the donkey, were stabled when I arrived. That Winter of 1947 remains legendary in Ireland to this day. After my tour of inspection I'm about to go and slide on a small, frozen-over pool, when I see a head peeping round the corner of the Old House. When he sees I've noticed him, the scamp comes forward. "Hello", he says, "I'm Jack." "Hello", says I, "I'm Herbert". Jack Staid was the son of the neighbour: our properties adjoined. After this brief introduction we became inseparable friends – and remain friends right up to the present day.

Jack, called by his nickname Studeen, taught me everything an Irish country lad could and should know. In return I could only tell him about Germany, and try to convince him that street-cars ran on electricity.

Straight off Jack took me home. The word had gone round Ballinlough that Mae Nally would be bringing a German boy back from her trip to Dublin, and everyone was curious to get a look at me. All the Staids were gathered: Jack's mother, who was smoking a cigarette; his father, nicknamed Navvy, who was puffing his pipe; Beatrice and Anne, his older sisters; and Jim, his older brother. There's a great meeting of minds, a cup of tea, a lot of friendliness, much cordiality, a lot of questions are asked of the new neighbour.

Finally Jack says "Let's go down the road to meet our friends" and we whizz off. Past my farm we go, past the neighbouring farm over the road. Jack tells me that this is Martin Nevin's and that there are two fellow-pupils here but, he adds, they're girls, we can say hello to them later. We call into James Moran. He's our age, but already built like an Irish oak and a head taller than us. Greetings; confab; we go on. We're aiming for the Halligans': Martin and his sister Celia - my future friends and school-mates; their sisters and brothers are older.

Then, on the way back, into the Nevins': Martin Nevin, who had three daughters, was a stocky man with quicksilver in his veins. He turned out to be a real wag, with whom you could have a real laugh and who was always up to something.[59]). Martin's daughters were Anne and Margaret, the latter being the younger one. Anne, the same age as me, often wore her hair as a thick, long plait – and I liked her. But she was so mischievous: there was no getting back at her.

In short, early in the morning, going to school, the Halligans would whistle for James Moran, and then together they'd do the same for the Nevin girls, then all of them for me, and finally the lot of us for Jack.

We were the Ballinlough Gang.

28

The Blizzard

A day or two later I was due to start school. But, that night, as we were sitting around the fire, a storm was brewing. The howling, whining and roaring down the chimney was so loud that I was really frightened. Eugene had the lucky idea of bringing in two more bags of turf before the storm worsened into a hurricane. The blizzard raged all night and when we got up next morning we were completely snowed in. The front of our house, facing North-South, took the full brunt of the North-Westerly storm. Here all the windows were snowed-up, and, when we opened the door, we looked at a hard-packed wall of snow – there was no way of even guessing how solid it was. Eventually we had to open the lower half of the window in the extension at the back, which was in the lee of the storm. Then we had to use the small ash-shovel to excavate the snow, bringing it into the bedroom first, until we'd made a hole big enough to crawl through.

We were faced with a sight which was as awe-inspiring as it was overwhelming. The farm buildings were snowed in right to the roof in places and the countryside was flattened out by the snow: not a ditch to be seen. The cattle were lowing in their stalls, the unmilked cow was mooing, the pigs were squealing, and Charlie could be heard kicking the wall – but there was no quick way of getting in to the animals. It wasn't till the late afternoon that we could do the milking and feed the livestock. Using our bare hands and the ash-shovel, it took us over an hour just to reach the shed-door to get out the shovels and spade. We had to search for the turf reek, a pyramid at least 3 metres in height. The pig-sty was between the cow-stable and the Old House: its door had been pushed in by the blizzard and the poor pigs were all on top of each other in the only snow-free corner of their quarters, all the rest being packed with compressed snow.

In the event it was around three weeks before we were able to move around freely in the open again. Nearly the whole country, and certainly the West coast, was virtually paralysed for several weeks. Us farmers came off best, being self-sufficient! And - the Nallys had nothing but praise for me: good boy! I'd passed the test, despite my short pants and legs frozen blue. (In my time it was unheard of, at least in the countryside, for boys to wear long trousers before Confirmation.) The 1947 Blizzard has become legendary in Ireland and a favourite topic of conversation, then as now and one in which I can, much to my satisfaction, chip in my recollections.

29

Tawny Lake

After the snow had melted I undertook an inspection of 'our' fields. The ones in front of the house stretched down to Tawny Lake, the first glimpse of which put me into a rapture of delight. A lake right in front of my front door – my dream of country life was fulfilling itself to the last detail.

Yet Tawny Lake is by no means typical of the classic Irish inland waters, the Loughs – either in size or features. Instead, Tawny Lake is quite narrow, extended and shallow. It's partly fed by a modest spring, but mainly by water draining down into it and that affects the amount of sediment in it. Most of it is so shallow that the grass in the surrounding cattle meadows continues into the lake as an uninterrupted carpet.

As Tawny Lake would quickly warm up in the Summer, it was sheer joy to wade through its knee-high, tepid waters, feet caressed by the pleasantly soft bottom. There was only one spot where you could swim properly, in the middle up at Golding's place: but I was the only one in our group of friends who could swim.

All year round there was a population of swans, partridges, mallards, and teal, but in the Spring whole flocks of migrating birds would come to rest on it. Something like 180 kinds of bird fly to Ireland, and quite a few of them would use Tawny Lake as a staging post. Jack and I would often sit on the low stone wall separating our lower meadow from the edge of the lake and watch the bright bustle of the birds. Absolutely unforgettable: the curlews flitting to and fro, nervously poking about on the soft shore of the lake with their long, curved beaks; and the smell of mint, which grew all over the shore area. In after years, when I dreamt of Ireland, Tawny Lake was always in the dream.

Low water in Tawny Lake: later it filled again. The Nally fields are on the left at the far back.

30

Facefield National School

It was finally time to start school. Mae escorted me and handed me over to the School Principal, Mister Malachy Garvey, and in turn he brought me to my class-mistress, Mrs. Forde. She taught Classes One to Four in one room, while Mr. Garvey took the Fifth to the Eighth in another. Once more I was stared at with unbounded curiosity, by teachers and pupils alike: the latter followed the introduction with interest and standing around us in a circle. A German in Facefield National School: that was something!

The pupils of Facefield National School 1948. Back row, from left: Christie Nevin (†), Gerald French, Jack Staid, Martin Halligan, Paddy Kennedy, Liam Gannon (†), Francis O'Dea (†), ? , Seamus Gannon, James Moran, Herbert Remmel, Peter Murray, ? , Headmaster Malachy Garvey. Second row from back, first from left Celia Halligan.

Mrs. Forde again gave me a place of honour on a school-bench at the back, and again I was to get free periods – but I also had cause for dissatisfaction. I'd been put in the Fourth Class, probably in the belief that I wouldn't be able to follow the teaching on account of the language. They didn't know about my time at Inchicore. But after a few weeks I was switched to Mr. Garvey's class, and sat next to my friend, Jack.

For me the first weeks at school are associated with chattering teeth and hands frozen blue, for each of the two class-rooms was only heated – or more accurately, slightly warmed – by an intermittent open fire – and this miserable breath of warmth was mainly of benefit to the teacher's back. The parents would take it in turns to bring in a donkey-cart load of turf, and it wasn't always the dry sods which found their way to the school. Before lessons began in the mornings, there'd sometimes be a tussle for the two 'stoker' jobs, because the lighting process could be dragged out, so that a whole lesson could be over before delicate flames started licking the sods. Two stokers were needed because they had to take it in turn to blow at the fire as long and as hard as possible. Once the flames began to blaze, the bottles of milk which we'd lined up in front of the open fire started to warm up. We brought them to school with our bread and butter.

School began at nine o'clock in the morning and finished at 3 o'clock. Facefield National School was founded in 1892, but the present school – a one-storeyed, right-angled building – dated from 1920. One side of the building was turned into a Church in the 1930s, when the third class-room wasn't needed any more because of a bit of a down-turn in the numbers of

"I am a farmer Boy on dis"

104

farmers' children. Until then the pupils had to re-arrange the class-room for Sunday Mass.

Schoolmaster Malachy Garvey performed prodigious pedagogic feats, teaching four classes in one room. While the fifth-formers sat on their benches, tussling with 'hard' mathematical tasks, the pupils in the eighth class would be gathered at farthest end of the room, in front of a giant map of the world, solving geographical problems. But if we glanced back at the benches behind us, we could see Seamus Gannon tugging Nancy O'Dea's pony-tail, and her brother, Francis, shooting small paper-balls into Nonie Cleary's Wellingtons with perfect accuracy. But if such learning-derailments from geographical and other lessons were detected, Mister Garvey would draw his cane over boyish palms, a painful honour which I was to experience not too rarely. But soon my favourite subjects were Composition and Reading.

A photograph of me has survived. It was taken by a travelling photographer, who went round all the schools in the County. I'd sent the photo home to my parents and written on the back, bilingually (!) : *"Ich binn Ein Bauern junge hire"* and "I am a Farmer Boy on dis". Clearly my German was diminishing; and if all my early English compositions shared this orthographic quality, then in retrospect I'm no longer surprised at the way Teacher Garvey ruffled his hair when he gave me back my early essays. Nevertheless, I'm grateful to my teacher in Ireland, and to the good old country school. It stands to their credit that, after going back to Germany, I never had the feeling of being behind educationally: on the contrary. And there is one thing for which I rate Facefield School particularly highly: my introduction to reading.

Our reading textbook in Facefield was a fairly ambitious literary novel in a school edition. It was about a Scottish mercenary who gets mixed up in the conflicts of Elizabethan Ireland. Though a 'cloak and dagger' story, it has literary value. We went through Maurice Walsh's *Blackcock's Feather* chapter by chapter – and we were practising reading, learning words, and coming to terms with punctuation, along with Irish history. I gobbled up this old book and re-read it so often that I can still recite its first paragraph from memory: "This is the story of me, David Gordon, and I will begin it on that day in May when I walked down the quay-wall at Mouth of Avon below Bristol and held discourse with one Diggory, sailing-master of the 'Speckled Hind'. – I begin it on that day because it was on that day life began for me." The day I first laid hand on *Blackcock's Feather* was the day when the world of literature opened for me.

Now, in my time, the stock of books in Irish farmhouses was meagre indeed, apart from the Bible and prayer-books. Once I'd been bitten by the reading bug, I was constantly on the look-out for books, or for anything to read. No farmhouse within a 3–4 kilometre radius was safe from my cadging for books. I read everything there was in the way of books, though certainly not taking all of it in. In the tiny town of Balla, a full six kilometres from Ballinlough, I ordered a comic, which appeared every fortnight I believe and cost a full three pence: *The Rover*. The hero of the never-ending, illustrated, serialised, stories was Rory of the Hill, a Scot fighting the odious English. On alternate Thursdays, rain, storm or shine, I'd march to Balla, cutting through the fields, to collect my periodical. By the time I was back home I'd the whole thing read.

Christie Nevin, my class-mate and undoubtedly the cleverest boy in the school, who had the makings of an intellectual, shared my hunger for books, and there wasn't a book we didn't exchange and discuss. I was deeply shocked and saddened when I revisited my old school for the first time in 1990 and was shown around the school-rooms, and naturally the Church as well, by Anne Duggan, a former class-mate and present head-mistress. I was devastated to see on a plaque set into the wall: "In memory of Christie Nevin, killed in Vietnam". Christie had emigrated to the USA, signed up, and been deployed to Vietnam. Granted wedding-furlough, he was leaving the front-line when he was killed. Christie was the first Irish-born American victim of the Vietnam War!

At some point we had visitors from America: Eugene and Mae's brother and sister. Peggy asked me what I wanted her to send from America. Books! And she sent me three: *Treasure Island, Moby Dick,* and *The Mystery Of The Red Triangle,* a Western. I had my first treasury of books.

I shared Eugene's bedroom in the extension: we each had our own bed. Apart from the fact that Eugene snored like a lion, I wanted my own bedroom, so that I could read in bed. Up under the roof, above the pantry, there was a room which remained unplastered: it did have a bed, but it was only used in extremis to put up visitors. The attic room was really basic: with no ceiling, you could see the roof timbers and the back of the roof-slates. But in the end my endless entreaties were granted and I was allowed to move up there. A bed, a tiny bedside cupboard, and a conceded candle – that was it. I was ecstatic to have my own kingdom. I could read as late as I wanted, and from my little window in the mornings I had the most beautiful view of the mountain, always a shimmering green. Al-though 855 feet (c 300 metres) in height, and several miles wide reaching from Balla to Kiltimagh, we never called it by the official name Sliabh Cairn, it just was "the mountain".

But there's one thing in connection with Facefield School which still angers me today: that I agreed to be excused lessons in Irish. Gaelic, the native language which the British came close to eradicating, is a compulsory subject in all Irish schools, and mastering it is a condition of entry into the public service. But it's spoken as an everyday language only in Gaeltacht areas, mainly situated in the West of Ireland, in Connaught, in Donegal and Kerry. While my class-mates struggled with Irish, I was allowed to do my own work.

I did acquire a stock of Gaelic words: a greeting phrase; an insult; and lots of words in everyday farm use. But there was one word which I particu-larly liked and used frequently in a perfect accent: *"anseo"* which I'd shout out loudly when teacher Garvey went through the attendance register. To give an example of the complexity of Gaelic – which lacks the letters, and thus also the sounds, for j, k, q, v, w, x, y, and z. The greeting phrase "how are you?" is written: *"Cén chaoi a bhfuil tú."* But it's pronounced Kee'he will tuu? This greeting is amusing if it's translated literally. Then it says: "What – the way which you are?" But how much pleasanter than the rude German challenge, *"Leck mich am Arsch!"* is the Gaelic equivalent:

With Eugene at the gable of our Old House, 1994. Notice the concrete rain tank, my "open air bathroom", and the little window of my bed- and reading-room.

"Pog mo hón!" It goes without saying that this charming phrase immediately entered my modest Gaelic vocabulary – and was frequently used, purely because it sounded so nice.

Along with the lessons, Facefield School offered a lot of fun and many diversions. The school yard was divided into sections for boys and girls by a low concrete wall. There were the maddest football-battles in the boys' yard, played barefoot and, with no leather ball, we used a hurling ball, or even sometimes a small sponge ball. One time, given a free kick, instead of kicking the ball I hit a stone below it: A terrible pain in my big toe, which Granny soothed with hot whiskey and a salve of butter. If a game of Catch was played, there was a wild hunt – over the concrete walls and round the school building, mowing down everything in the way. The pupils in the lower classes would squeeze into a corner of the playground for safety's sake. There, penned like sheep, they'd anxiously watch the chasing.

It was a particular honour to be allowed to fetch the teachers' tea-water from Tony's Well, a spring in the field.

But nicest of all was the walk to and from school. Early, our Ballinlough Gang gathered up Jack Staid, it was downhill to McEveney's Farm, and then we'd branch to the right at Cruckaun Doite, a narrow sunken boreen

The Boreen Cruckaun Doite. The elves lived in the white-thorn ahead.

almost totally overgrown with Whitethorn, a place which felt really eerie to me – and not just because of the fairies, elves, and other mystical beings which did their mischief here.

We'd often meet up with the Townalough Gang here, and we'd continue down the Boreen with them, past Murphy's farm, where we'd often come upon old Mrs. Murphy, dunging out the pig-sty with her bare hands. Then it was through the middle of Joyce's Farm and up the hill past Tony's Well, right up to the school itself.

On 1st April our shoes would fly into the corner, and we'd go barefoot till the last day of October. In the mornings, if the hoar-frost was still in the meadows and a thin layer of ice on the pools of water, we'd be on the look-out to see if the McEveney or Murphy cows and cattle were already let out. If the fresh cow-pats were steaming in the morning cold, then there was nothing like diving over the ditch and putting our feet, frozen numb, into the pleasant warm cow-shit. And we wouldn't be the only ones sitting on the school benches with green-stained feet in the mornings.

On our way home, as we passed, the farmers working in the fields would call, "the school-children are coming" – seeing us, they could be fairly sure that it was about three o'clock in the afternoon. The McEveney brothers – Mike, Jim and Paddy, three fellows in their mid-twenties built like trees – would also have espied us, and would often hide behind the ditch. As we passed they'd jump out howling like bannshees, and try to catch us and scrub our faces with their wiry three-day beards. "You'll have met the

McEveneys" would be Granny's laconic comment if I got home with tomato-red cheeks.

We had great fun with the mother of the three boys, old Mrs. McEveney – who was always trembling with curiosity and who had never been further than Balla or Castlebar. Often, as she saw us coming, she'd quickly bring out her three-legged stool and sit down in front of her farm-gate and wait for us. "God bless you, Herbert! Now tell me, Are the fields in Germany green?" "Certainly, Mrs. McEveney, not like in Ireland, but the fields in Germany are green too." "Well, Herbert, isn't it grand, what a beautiful world God has made. But now, tell me Herbert, do the hens in Germany also lay eggs?"

Skipping school was an absolute necessity in Facefield, and extensively tolerated by the teachers. After all, they knew that even the hands of ten-, eleven-, and twelve-year old scamps were often badly needed on the farms, particularly at sowing- and harvest-time. When Facefield School celebrated its centenary in 1992, Anne Duggan, the headmistress, took the trouble to dig out the old school records, including the old attendance Registers. How surprised I was that, for some months, there was a clear preponderance of absent strokes by my name.

A story used to be told again and again of something that happened before my time. A teacher, cycling to school in the morning, sees a notorious truant flit across the road and disappear into a cornfield. When he reaches the spot, the teacher calls into the cornfield, "Are you in there, John Kennedy?" – "No, Sir", comes the reply.

The priest used to come into school, quite officially, and interrupt the lesson to test pupils on the Catechism: that was completely outside my experience, either in Germany or in Inchicore. At any rate, it wasn't rare for Father Lowry to turn up and take a Catechism lesson. When the answer wasn't known, or was wrong, the cane would sometimes dance. The questions and answers were set out in a school edition of the Catechism and we had to learn them off by heart, word-perfect. "What does Amen mean?" "Amen means so be it." "Good, good, Herbert, sit down." And Father Lowry would beam.

I joined in whole-heartedly, and not just with learning the Catechism. In Facefield, it was customary for pupils, from the 6th class on I think, to gradually prepare to assist the priest on the altar. A whole row of up-and-coming, but inactive, altar-boys would kneel around the podium of the small altar in the Church-room at Facefield. The idea was that, by watching, they'd gradually absorb the Mass-ritual and learn how to serve. As far as I recall, there was no theoretical instruction. (In those days the Catholic Mass was still in the old liturgy: all in Latin, with incense and tinkling of bells, with *Kyrie-Eleison* and *Tantum Ergo Sacramentum*, and the priest having his back to the nave.) At any one point there'd only be two lads

Meeting the old neighbours at Facefield Church: Saying Hello to Mrs. Murphy. Jack Staid on the left. Front right Margret Nevin. (The author's wife and daughter are in the bakground.)

from 8th class actually serving Mass and wearing the robes. And they'd be jealously on the look-out, lest one of the eleven trainees might try to perform some of the duties which were rightfully theirs, such as ringing the bell. I would eventually also have become an altar-boy, but by 8th class I was to be back in Germany.

Landscape at Ballinlough village, viewed from Croagh Mòr. In the background Celia Halligan's Farm. (Please don't mind the cluster of litter lodged by one of my Ballinlough neighbours, bottom left!)

110

By the way, after returning to Cologne I continued my Catholic way of life at first, immediately reporting to Father Adelkamp in Höhenhaus, who received me with open arms. Knowing that the son of a well-known local Communist and Atheist was being embraced in the arms of his Church, he must have felt quite triumphant. Father let me get on with it (the boy has to strike his own path). But more than that: Mother washed and starched my altar-boy robes, which I proudly carried to Church over my arm on Sundays. Old Adelkamp was even more enchanted by the idea that I'd been an altar-boy in Catholic Ireland, and I was immediately enrolled into the circle of Höhenhaus ministrants – called Minis nowadays. That my incarnation as an Irish altar-boy was only passive he didn't know and I'd forgotten to tell him. The long and the short of it was that an altar-boy dropped out and I was to serve Sunday Mass. With no training in the practical side, the whole thing turned into a disaster. During Mass – I think it was between the preparing of the altar and the washing of hands – the Missal had to be carried over from the right side of the altar to the left, or vice-versa. In any case, I blundered and picked the wrong time to take up the lectern with the Missal on it to carry it to the other side of the altar. Passing the tabernacle, a genuflection was prescribed.

While doing that I saw the priest going over to the side of the altar from which I'd just taken the book. But he noticed that I was on my way to the wrong side of the altar and turned back, while I'd started bring the Missal back to its old position. In short: we passed each other and Father Adelkamp had to do another about-turn. No question: this was my first and only sortie as a serving altar-boy in Höhenhaus Church. It's likely that Pastor Adelkamp saw my mishap as an act of Communist sabotage. Cousin Betty, who was at that Mass, still speaks of my debut today.

Going to confession was the big problem of my Catholic life in Ireland. Of course I knew what real sins were, but I was never convinced that I'd committed any. As even Jack couldn't help me here, I had to help myself. So I confessed all sorts of miscellaneous rubbish to poor Father Lowry: That I'd been swearing and using bad words; that I'd lied; that I'd watched the bull at his business with the cow and wondered how men and women did it. Indeed, my school-friend, Mary Garvey, who was some classes above me and later married my teacher Malachy Garvey, today still vehemently insists that I explained that intimate technique to the girls in the class – which I equally vehemently deny. According to the gravity of my sins, Father Lowry would thunder out, ten Ours Fathers and five Hail Marys, or the other way round. And after that I was free of sin.

31

Daily Life In Ballinlough

I was fortunate to arrive at the Nallys' in Ballinlough at the beginning of the farm year in February. It meant I had the chance, not just to observe all the agricultural work through the seasons, but also to take an active part in it. In my time the way the fields and meadows to the front and rear of the house were used always stayed the same. The fields behind the house were always used for grazing because of the slope; two of the front fields were hay-meadows; and another was used to grow potatoes.

A field is generally an area of about one hectare (c. two-and-a-half acres) at most, usually enclosed by the ditch: an earthen wall, overgrown with thorny broom. (In English usage a ditch is a trench, but in Ireland, for reasons that are unknown to me, the earth-wall is called a ditch, while the hole excavated to build the ditch is called the dyke.) Where there are plenty of stones, dry-stone walls would generally form the enclosure. This field-structure, with its handkerchief-sized fields and enclosing ditches, has continued over generations and is characteristic for nearly the whole of Ireland. I can't recall ever seeing a barbed-wire fence in my part of Ireland, or even a wooden one.

The first job I did with Eugene was to repair the ditch where the cattle had found gaps in the thorny furze and forced their way through to the neighbouring field to get at juicier grass. These gaps, called "break-throughs", would be blocked with grass-sods, which we dug up and stacked up neatly on top of each other. Then we'd hack branches off the thorny-furze and line the crown of the repair with them, with the tips facing into the meadow, and after that we'd weigh down the whole with more grass-sods. Doing the Fence wasn't pleasant work, especially as working gloves were unknown and thorns would get into your hands.

The next job was bringing the manure from the stable out to the area where the hay was to be grown and also to where the potatoes and oats were to be. White cabbage, carrots, and lettuce were cultivated in the garden behind the barn. No other vegetables were grown in my time, indeed were scarcely known. For shifting the manure Charlie was hitched to the two-wheeled horse cart.

These were in use all over Ireland and farmers set great store on their colour scheme: the body of the wagon was usually blue; wheel-rims, spokes and shaft were mostly magenta-red. The two wheels of the horse cart were secured with a single iron peg, knocked into a long hole bored into the axle, and of course it did not fit in to the millimetre. The knocking of the hub on the axle was a characteristic of Irish horse carts and each had its own individual sound.

If Eugene was on his way home on our horse cart on a calm day, we'd

Springtime ploughing in Ireland

hear the knocking of our cart from a long way away. Four-wheeled horse carts were rare and farm-wagons *(Ackerwagen/Leiterwagen)*, such as are general in Germany, completely unknown.

The horse harness consists of a bridle, collar, belly-band, crupper (breechings), and straddle – the underside of which is cushioned. Above is attached a driving-rod, which we usually greased with butter. This takes a chain which in turn is fastened to the left and right onto the shafts of the cart. Consequently, part of the weight of the cart rests on the horse's back, for which reason there has to be care to spread the weight evenly during loading.

Loading the cart with manure was miserably hard work, as was the spreading of it with a four-pronged dung-fork, called a Graeps. I would spread it after school was over – and I soon got fed up to the nose with that. It was practically a tradition that youngsters got stuck in, spreading the muck with the fork – and it was certainly not held in bad odour as child labour.

One day Eugene disappeared on his bike: he'd gone to his brother Martin's at Belcarra and came back with Martin's mare. Eugene wanted to plough up two fields rented up at Black Jack's and sow them with oats: till then they'd been used as meadows. One horse wouldn't suffice for this bit of ploughing. On the next morning, clear and sunny, Charlie was hitched up, Martin's mare was tied to the cart behind, the harrow and the single-bladed

Harrow

113

iron swing plough – consisting of sock, coulter, board, and ploughshare – were loaded, and off we went to Black Jack's. I'd never seen horse-ploughing before and was full of enthusiasm! With this simple iron plough, and without a guidance-wheel in front, Eugene was able to plough absolutely straight furrows. The coulter cut the ground with a hiss and the board turned the thick strip of shiny black earth. The first sea-gulls on the search for worms followed with their harsh cries, and the pleasant smell of freshly-opened earth hung in the air. [60]

This was my dream-world! Even looking back, after all these years, I can feel the infinite stillness of that translucent, sunny March day, only broken by the sound of the plough, the snorting of the horses, the jubilation of the larks in the sky above, and the occasional screams of the gulls.

At six o'clock came the distant ring of the Angelus Bell from Balla Church – knocking-off time. After the final bit of Black Jack's was ploughed the next day, and Eugene had prepared the seed-bed with the harrow, he sowed the oats from a sling around his neck, using his hand. Then he showed me how the harrowing – only Charlie drew the harrow – was managed. Thereupon he swung himself onto his bike, caught hold of the mare and set off to bring her back to Martin. I could scarcely believe it: he was leaving me to drill the oats on my own. As for Charlie – who really didn't accept a person of my size at the time – he was well-disposed towards me on that day and willingly obeyed every light tug on the rein, so I'd no problems. Up the field, down the field, across the field up, and across the field down: it worked perfectly. I thought of my parents, my brother at home in Cologne: if only they could see me now. Herbert, entirely on his own, working a field with a horse! Eugene gets back, checks, is satisfied. Well done, good boy!

32

The Holy Potato

Granny's sitting in front of the Old House on a stool, a huge basket of potatoes beside her. She takes a potato out of the basket, cuts it in pieces and drops them into a second basket. So it goes on, potato after potato. Granny explains to me that it's wasteful to put a whole potato into the furrow as a seed-potato. It's enough to cut out each eye (a *skillaun*) and plant that. At any rate, that's how they did it all over Ireland, and I'd see what a crop there'd be.

So I run down the furrow dropping in *skillauns* at regular intervals, measured by eye, out of a buckled-on flat basket. I'm rushing because

Eugene's suggested that, for fun, we should race to see who finishes his row first. Sometimes I'd win.

Nevertheless, guiding the drill-plough, which closes up the dressed furrows, that was Eugene's domain.

Later, when the potatoes sprouted leaves, they'd have to be sprayed against potato-blight *(phytophthora infestans)*. Incidentally, this was the

only chemical (fungicide) applied to crops during my time in Ireland. And, certainly, Irish farmers performed no other task so meticulously as spraying the potato foliage. And there was good reason for that: Between 1844 and 1848 the potato-blight raged all over Ireland, leading to the greatest Hunger catastrophe in Irish history because potatoes was what they mainly lived on. The Great Famine caused the starvation of about one million Irish people, and led to an unimaginable impoverishment of the countryside. On top of that, it precipitated the flood of emigration – resembling a flight – of more than two million Irish people, mainly to America. Together, these two events reduced the population of the country from about 6 millions in the middle of the 19th century to about 2.8 millions by the end. There are

very many ruins of farm-cabins, abandoned because of the Hunger, all around the country, particularly in the County of Mayo. Even in my time Ireland only had something like 2.6 million inhabitants. Right down to this day every Irishman and Irishwoman is aware of The Great Famine, the country's greatest tragedy.

Two or three days before the spraying, wooden barrels had to be brought to the edge of the potato-field. Small sacks of sky-blue, water-soluble fungicide crystals [61] would be suspended into them. Naturally there was no tanker, so I'd the task of filling the barrels with water. Another wooden barrel would be put on the donkey-cart (also called the ass-cart, which was a smaller version of the horse-cart), which I'd drive to our rain-water reservoir at the gable-end of the house. After filling up, I'd drive back to the field and pour the water out into the barrels.

The Famine: a family searching for the last potatoes

115

During the journey I was hard put to it to hold the cask steady, to stop it tipping over. A sack was tied across the top of the barrel to stop the water slopping out. Our donkey knew the way without the reins, but did everything possible to thoroughly infuriate me. Every time a pothole, an unevenness, or a dip, came in sight, he'd abandon the wheel-tracks and steer towards the mischief, making the cart jump, hop and tilt and forcing me to perform wild dances in an effort to hold the barrel upright. My raging and shouting helped not at all. I wasn't able to let go of the barrel to give him a belt – as the donkey seemed to know very well. He'd wiggle his ears and look out for the next hole. But, on the way back, the damned beast would stay exactly on track.

Eugene did the spraying work with a back pack sprayer.

Even before the Autumn potato harvest – and even before the stalks had withered – we'd dig up new potatoes for our meals. If Granny charged me with digging up "some new spuds" for the midday meal, I'd get onto it right away. I'd grab a pail, shoulder the three-pronged dung-pike and be off to the potato field. I'd set the pike behind a potato plant and dig up the ground, and it was an exciting lottery every time: how many potatoes had it made; how big were they? And when I saw the gleaming, well-rounded and usually big potatoes in the freshly-dug and scented earth, a feeling of content would always steal over me. So that is what became of the tiny bits of potato, each with its eye, which we'd set in the Spring. That was a miracle as far as I was concerned.

But harvesting the potatoes was not quite as wonderful: pulling up and gathering potatoes with icy fingers in wind-driven rain. Earlier Eugene would have broken up the rows of potatoes with the plough. Before all of

Working the potato pit

that, we'd have dug a potato-pit somewhere at the edge of the field: it was around five-six metres long, two metres wide and some 60 cm. deep. We'd empty the baskets of potatoes into it until there was a pyramid of potatoes about a metre high. This would be covered with straw and earth thrown over it.

As the Winter went on, we'd take potatoes for ourselves and the pigs from this pit every day. It wasn't too far from the house, as potatoes were always set in a field close to home.

All through the Winter I'd have to do with the potatoes we'd harvested in the Autumn, as I was responsible for getting the feed for the pigs ready. The big fireplace had been kept on in the 'old house', along with its crane from which an enormous and really heavy cast-iron three-legged pot would be hung. I'd fill the pot with potatoes right to the brim, add water and cover it with an old sack and then its heavy cast-iron lid. I was scarcely able to hang the empty pot onto the gallows, let alone lift it when full. Having hung up the empty pot over the turf-fire, I'd toil away, filling it with water and potatoes. Eugene would often come and watch, doubled up with laughter at the laborious way I was doing the job: "Well, well, my boy, you're not such a big strong German after all. We'll have to feed you up a bit more!"

But, after the potatoes were done, I'd have to call Eugene to bring down the pot – which was no simple job for him either. Then I'd stand by and take the rise out of him.

To the boiled potatoes was added a proper measure of oatmeal (crushed oats), along with all the kitchen waste. While this was going on, the pigs could smell their food cooking and were squealing for all they were worth.

Every day we'd have potatoes for dinner, in one of two forms: potatoes boiled in their skins or mashed potatoes. This was different to what I was used to. At home we'd have 'salted potatoes', meaning they were peeled and salted whilst being boiled. But I soon came to terms with the Irish 'jacket potatoes' and the dexterity needed to peel them with my fingers.

I immediately noticed a difference between the way food was served in Germany and in Ireland. At home the food was served in dishes – at least it was before provisions ran short. There'd be a dish for potatoes, another for vegetables, another for meat and one for the gravy. We'd take as much as we wanted. But now either Granny or Mae would hand out plates of food. At first I thought that it was the portion I was expected to eat and that I mustn't leave any. So I'd keep stuffing food into myself long after I was full, and still finding that the plate wasn't empty. That is why I soon rounded out and put on weight in Ireland.

When Granny or Mae handed us a plate of steaming potatoes, it was sheer bliss to spike up a potato with your fork, peel away the skin, cut the hot potato into pieces, sprinkle salt on them, and crown them with a good knob of butter: that was absolutely delicious.

Even though I'd come to Ireland on account of the great hunger in Germany, I've only faded memories of what was served at midday meals. Since coming to Ireland, being able to eat until I was full had become so normal that hunger only came into my mind when my thoughts drifted towards Cologne.

I can remember ham, cabbage and potatoes; bacon, cabbage and potatoes; ribs, cabbage and potatoes; and cabbage with mashed potatoes. Now and then there'd be a boiled or roasted chicken with cabbage and potatoes. If Mae had been in town that morning, she sometimes brought home some beef: then there'd be steak, cabbage and potatoes: but that was very rare.

I can only smack my lips at the thought of the other Irish victuals: rashers, sausages, fried eggs, soda bread and butter for breakfast – deeply enjoyable. Currant bread baked by Granny likewise.

On cold Winter mornings, when the house hadn't warmed up and I'd come in with my teeth chattering from my morning ablutions out at the gable water-butt, Granny would have a dish of steaming porridge ready on the table for us. Although porridge is only oat-flakes cooked in water, it is really enjoyable in the Winter and it heats you right through. I'd heap up the porridge into a little hill on the plate, make a dent in the top and put a knob of butter in it. Cold milk would then be poured over it all, and plenty of sugar on top of that: wonderful!

Another treat became an evening ritual for Eugene and me. Sitting at the fire after the work was done and I'd finished my homework, but before Eugene was ready to 'go visiting', we'd only need to look at each other to know: it's time for sops. In a trice a pot of milk was heated on the turf fire, poured into mugs, soda bread broken into it and a good measure of sugar added. We'd have our simple sops nearly every night, sitting around the fire comfortable and contented, telling stories.

If anyone had talked to us about organic produce in those days, we'd have looked at him in puzzlement. Our fare then, admittedly simple, was as pure as nature and completely organic.

We did not know of chemical fertilisers, and pigs stuffed with antibiotics were inconceivable – as was the idea of cattle fed on fish-and-bone-meal, and cows with poisoned brains staggering around the fields as though drunk.

Indeed, during my nearly three years in Ballinlough, I cannot remember one animal dying of disease within the vicinity and several kilometres around. The only veterinary medication in the house was a large bottle of castor oil. Once we had a bullock with colic. I had to hold the beast firm, keeping my thumb over one nostril and my index and middle finger over the other, pressing the two together as hard as I could. Then the beast went absolutely quiet, allowed its mouth to be opened, and let Eugene stick the castor oil bottle well down its gullet and pour in half. The beast soon shed its colic but it was advisable to stay well away from its rear end for a while.

33

A Day in The Bog

The oats sown, the potatoes set, grass growing in the hay-meadows, and the cattle contenting themselves on the explosive growth of fresh, juicy greenery – time for a break on the farm?

One morning there's a busy to-and fro-ing: Granny has a Soda Bread in the Pot Oven and Mae's packing a big basket. Into it goes an old cast-iron water-kettle, totally black with soot; also a soot-black tea-pot; a sooty conserve-tin; half a dozen fresh eggs; a crock of butter; a tin box of tea; another of sugar; a bottle of milk; and an aluminium jug holding about five litres of water into which a few handfuls of oat-meal have been thrown – a superbly refreshing drink!

Granny takes the soda bread, smelling heavenly, out of the pot oven, lets it cool a little, then wraps the still warm bread and adds it to the basket with the utensils. Eugene has already put out a singular spade: a piece of iron forged onto its plane, low down, on the right-hand corner: making something in the shape of an uneven-sided triangle. This is a turf-spade, invariably known by its Gaelic name, *Sléan* (pronounced shlawn). There's also a hatchet, a mattock, and a normal spade. I'm given the job of hitching up the ass. When the donkey sees the assembled equipment, he becomes docile and well-behaved. His ears prick forward inquisitively; it's off to the bog for turf-cutting, and he knows that this time the work won't be strenuous for him.

After the Spring field work, and after the April winds have dried the surface of the bogs to an extent, the sods of turf have to be cut for the Winter, for these usually need time to dry out: normally they're left until late Summer or beginning of Autumn, when they have to be brought home.

Our turf bank (called *portach* in Gaelic) isn't far from Townalough Village, something like a full half-hour's journey from our farm. On the

I bought this turfspade in a flea market in Germany. The blade seems to be of Irish origin, the handle is usual German. Unfortunately the seller had no idea where it came from.

way there we'd happen on neighbours, also on their way to the turf-cutting. Weather prophecies would be or there'd be comments on the day, with the satisfied observation, "a blessed weather today".

Cutting turf is heavy work which has to be executed in distinct stages. Bruised and blistered hands, a miserably painful spine, and exhausted leg-muscles are taken for granted. Nevertheless: during my time "a day in the bog" – despite all the very heavy labor – was a social event, a communal special occasion, of the very first rank. It was an indispensable part of the Irish psyche. Sean McCarthy, the writer, got it exactly right when he wrote: "The bog isn't a place, it's a feeling". (It must have been during our holiday in Ireland in 1994, while we were sitting with Jack Staid over a pint of Guinness in the little town of Balla, that a well-car of turf, its sides all decorated, was driven through the town by locals with loud whoops and much jubilation. The New York Irish community had decided to order a rail of original Irish "peat bog" to celebrate their heritage day. The well-wagon was freighted over to the USA and the Irish there were able to celebrate their "day in the bog" with real Irish turf. This goes to show how important this phenomenon is in the psyche of the Irish diaspora too.)

Arriving in the bog, the ass is unhitched and put on a long tether. We take up mattock and spade and start stripping away the surface growth ("fum" in Gaelic, mainly heather with its fiendish roots) from the area to be cut. The area needed to provide the turf for the coming Winter was never measured. Experience determined its size, and I cannot recall too little ever being cut.

Last year's cutting (the bog-hole) left a turf-bank with a vertical drop of a scant two metres in which water had accumulated over the Winter. The breadth of the segment now to be cut had to be estimated so as to enable the turf-cutter to lift the sod cut with his sléan "comfortably" up onto the bank, a maximum width of two metres (6 feet). Each sod would be about a foot or 30 centimetres square. As the cutting proceeded, and the cutter worked his way down, the layers would get lower and wetter, meaning that the cutter had to raise the wetter sods higher. Consequently the work got harder as it went along, with the heaviest effort coming near the end of the day.

Whilst Eugene – the cutter – cut and lifted the turf, I – the catcher (and spreader) – would have to get hold of the sods and lay them on the bank sufficiently far from the edge to allow room for the sods still to be cut. If there wasn't enough room, a roughly-made wooden wheelbarrow was at hand to carry the sods further away into the "hinterland" of the bank. This archaic monster of a wheelbarrow, its wheel entirely wooden, was itself so heavy that I could scarcely move it empty, let alone with its load of turf. So I preferred to take a few paces back with each sod of turf picked up.

Eugene, like the other farmers, liked to cut the turf at a steady, apparently slow rate, using just the pressure of his arms or torso to cut into the soft turf. Cut, upswing, place; cut, upswing, place; and so on, for hour after hour. For my part, I had to catch up the sod with my fork, take some paces back, and deposit it. Catch, pace back, deposit. There the sods would lie, in nice straight rows, to dry out. As I could never keep up with Eugene's pace, and was a downright poor catcher, the sods often piled up, higglety-piggelty, on the edge of the turf cutting. Eugene's dissatisfied look told me everything. You can imagine how relieved I was when Eugene suggested that I should light a good fire. It must have been about 1 o'clock – lunchtime! But I can't remember anyone ever bringing a watch to the bog.

When the fire's glowing red, Eugene swings himself out of his bog-hole, looks around and sounds three short whistles. The neighbours, in their turf-banks all around us, straighten up and stretch, pick up their baskets, walk over to us and sit down around the fire. I, with a neighbour's boy, have the job of gathering up the sooty black kettles and filling them at a nearby springwater hole – the water in which already looks very like the tea which is to be brewed. The kettles are put into the fire, where they join the equally sooty preserve-tins in which the eggs are boiled. The brewing up of the tea in the aluminium teapots follows, always on the principle of at least one spoon of tea for each person and one for the pot. To let the tea brew, the pot is also be set into the glowing embers. Finally Eugene sticks a little twiglet of gorse into the spout of the tea-pot to serve as a strainer. And so a black tea is brewed which is unsurpassed in flavour. Soda bread, butter, boiled eggs, possibly a slice of bacon (salami is unknown), tea, perhaps a sip of milk from the bottle – that's always our meal.

And it's hard to describe how much this simple fare was relished, the surroundings adding to the pleasure: A light, warm and velvety-soft wind from the Atlantic caresses the bog. Here and there the heather, drying in the sun, crackles; and the blossoming white filigree bog-cotton sways as in dance; turf-mosses form carpets of green, yellow, red, and orange; larks hang rejoicing in the blue heavens; lapwings show off their aerial acrobatics; snipes run around nervously; butterflies flutter; dragon-flies whirr; and the pleasant (at least to me), musty smell of fresh-cut turf mixes with the smoke and – a vista stretched far into the countryside.

An atmosphere only to be found here, in the Irish bog.

And, on top of all that, there's the get-together with the neighbours: chin-wagging, laughing, joking; stories about the latest night-encounter with the secretive fairies are told, with wholly credible elaboration. There'd be complaints about cattle prices, always too low; the achievements or performance of the Mayo (Gaelic) Football Team in the All-Ireland are passionately praised or damned to Hell, tears in their eyes. News is exchanged; and there's philosophising about the Irish world at home and the wide world out there. The night before this or that neighbour has been "visiting" one or other neighbour who has a radio. In my time not many had a radio – then called a "wireless". They were too expensive to buy and, with no electricity, they ran on wet-batteries which only lasted for a few hours. To charge them up, people had to go into town, which people didn't always have time to do: motor-cars were few and far between. So the neighbour who's heard the news the night before recites it, near-enough word-perfect. And then it's discussed, argued over, and God is begged to keep Ireland safe from the sins of the great wide world.

The first time at the bog, our more distant neighbours hardly know me. Some of them have seen me in Church, others have heard from their children about the German, loafing about in class. Now, here around the bog-fire, I'm overwhelmed with questions, have to speak up and answer: explain what the Bombing's like, the destroyed cities; and also have to listen to opinions about Nazi-Germany which I myself – ten years old – can't share, and hear reports about how, for instance, Rommel's Desert Foxes gave the English in Africa a proper roasting. Each tries to trump the other with stories about how Ireland, despite her neutrality, nevertheless helped the Germans in the War – though behind the scenes and illicitly (which naturally isn't so).

One neighbour says: "Of course we very secretly supplied German U-Boats with fuel somewhere near Cork or Limerick". Another comments, quite seriously: "Now I know why turf was scarce at the time!"

I'd lie in the middle of these Irish, racy of the soil, belonged with them, am accepted, feel at home: convince myself that I'm at least half-Irish. I could purr with well-being.

Footed turf

With the turf cut and spread, we'd often have to cycle out to the bog, depending on the weather, to turn the drying sods. (Mae often came with us.) Even if it rained continuously, the sods still had to be turned because, left lie too long, they'd revert to bog and be lost. Bend-

Sitting up high on the load of turf was the cherry on top

ing over to turn or 'foot' the turf was miserable, stooping, work, a veritable martyrdom for the spine. The Irish speak of back-breaking days in the bog. Once the sods have dried out a bit, it's back to the bog: this time to build small hollow pyramids through which the wind could blow and finally finish off the drying.

Then comes the next stage in the process. If the turf-bank's too far from the bog road, the hardened lane, and if the ground's too soft for horse and cart, then the turf has to be shifted to the side of the bog road by donkey – either using the lighter ass-cart or long baskets hung on either side of the donkey's back. There it's unloaded, to be brought home by horse and cart.

As the sods lose well over 80 per cent of their moisture-weight during the drying, the horse can take an awful lot more of them than would fit into the

Building the turf reek. Notice the horse's harness and the coloured cart.

ordinary car. So it's re-arranged by removing the wooden sides and replacing them with high, slatted cart rails. The sods are thrown into the cart until they reach the top of the rail. Then Eugene skilfully builds upwards, making a flat-topped pyramid to complete the load. My job's throwing up the sods. I'm allowed

123

2004: A nostalgic tour in the bog near Murneen / Kiltimagh: Claire and Tom Leydon along with me and my wife Karin

to sit on top of the pyramid on the way home. Bringing home the turf was the tops for me.

Sitting high up on the load of turf, with the characteristic knock of the cart axle in my ears, I could see over all the ditches and, from on high, would give a jovial greeting to all the woman neighbours who, curious to see who was on the approaching cart, had stepped out of their houses. Great fun. This was my world, but unfortunately I only had this experience three times – all the more unforgettable on that account.

At home the turf would be built up into a longish, even, towering pyramid.

Setting the outer layers of the Turf Reek involved a fair amount of skill, as it had to be fairly water-proof. Its construction marked the end of the Turf-Season: the cutting, footing, drawing, and stacking of the sods. People's backs could recover – until the following year.The next year we rented a turf-bank some five kilometres further away, as Townalough was turfed out. In contrast to my first year in the bog, the second was less pleasant, on account of the weather. Now I cursed and damned the bog: standing bent over, in the wind-whipped rain; freezing; shivering; moaning about my bad back and – nevertheless loving the bog. A day in the bog, that was something!

Nowadays the turf is mainly "cut" by machines, which run across the bog, trailing long circular sausages of turf (called "sausage turf" by the Irish). Nevertheless, many refuse to give up at least some of the back-breaking work of cutting the turf with the *sléan*, just for the sake of maintaining the old tradition of cutting the turf and to enjoy the unique atmosphere of the bog.

34

Hay-Making In Ballinlough

In my time there was scanty use of agricultural machinery, at least on small farms like ours. Our only mechanical appliances were the back-pump for spraying the potato-stalks, which I've already mentioned, and a horse-drawn McCormick mowing machine, which had a simple mowing bar without binding mechanism. But the mowing depended less on the mowing-machine than on the weather, and by June at the latest hay-making would come up in every conversation. When our priest, Father Lowry, prayed for good weather during Mass, he could be sure that the response of Amen from the congregation couldn't be more fervent and supplicant. What hay was saved determined whether cattle could be kept during the Winter or not, and so had a big effect on the level of income. Selling cattle and pigs was the only source of income for our small farmers, aside from a modest sale of eggs. This existential importance of hay is reflected in the language. We did not speak of bringing home the hay, but of saving the hay. And the same applied to the turf.

Because of the damp and warm – even wet and warm – conditions, the grass in the meadows would almost shoot up into the heavens. As chemicals were never used, Irish meadows were also thick with beautiful flowers. In my time the meadow-corncrakes were taken for granted. Now, with the use of machinery, they've nearly died out and strenuous efforts are being made to maintain what's left of them.

My job during the hay-making was to trot along beside the mowing machine, armed with a wooden hay-rake, always ready to use it if there was a blockage in the mowing-bar. Then it was a matter of poking and

Members of O'Connell family of Ballydesmond, Co. Cork, saving hay in the early 1950s. – Notice the men's trousers! (see page 154)

tugging until the mowing blade was free. Usually we'd have to borrow a second horse from a neighbour or from Martin as Charlie couldn't pull the machine at the required speed on his own. So thick was the grass that the blade would have to turn at a reasonable speed to have a chance of cutting through the jungle.

If the weather was fine, and there was a light Summer breeze, the upper side of the swathes would dry in a jiffy and they'd have to be turned. But if rain intervened, soaking the dried swathes and congealing them to the ground, we'd have to wait for the first patch of blue sky and use two-pronged hay-forks to shake out the swathes. Saving the hay was hard work and always meant big blisters on your hands.

However, in fine hot weather, which you also get in Ireland, I always worked with the upper part of my body bare (never getting sun-burnt), causing great amazement thereby. During my stay in Mayo I never saw a single farmer working bare-chested.

Once the hay was finally dry, it would be raked up: first into rows, then into tiny heaps called *crauers*, then into little hay-stacks, and ultimately into bigger ones: hay-cocks or -wynds.

Because strong and heavy Atlantic gales would blow over the country as well as soft Summer breezes, the hay-cocks would have to be storm-proofed. As hemp-rope, or other manufactured cords or lines were too dear and

126

so out of the question, the ropes for the cocks would be made out of twisted hay (*súgán*, pronounced sugawn). A wire bucket handle was stuck into a hollowed-out elder-branch and then bent into a crank shape; its protruding end was twisted into a loop.

To start the rope, long bits of smoothed-out hay were threaded through it. I had to turn the elder-branch crankshaft, while Eugene kept adding hay – just like spinning wool. In a trice a rope would be made, thrown over the cocks, then tied around the base with more rope – finished. The thing could also be done with a piece of stick or branch, but the twisting took longer. The wind never ruffled up a single one of our stacks, or blew it over.

McCormick-Deering horse drawn mowing machine

We had no float, but bringing in the hay was a simple affair on the meadows near the farm, such as the lower hay-meadow on Tawny Lake. The complications of loading and unloading the hay were avoided: a long towing-chain would be put around Charlie's collar, which would be put around the bottom of the hay cock and off he'd go: the stack would simply be dragged into the barn, much like draught-horse work in the German forest.

The hay cocks were manoeuvred as close as possible to the shed and then the hay was piked in, making a high pile. Piking the hay upwards was Eugene's job. Either Mae or myself would then take up the piked-up hay with our own forks and throw it to the back of the shed, where the other one would even it out and trample it down to make it more solid. This was heavy work, monotonous and dusty. And, when we slid down to the ground after the work was done, we looked like hay cocks ourselves and we felt prickly, itchy and

Dragging home the hay cock

sore all over; on top of that our hair was totally matted. I tried to alleviate this torture by jumping into the concrete rain tank at the gable end. But I also remember that two of the Mac lads, I think it was Jim and Mike, came to help out.

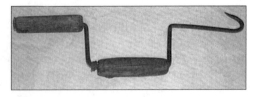

The twister

As Mae and I didn't have the strength and stamina to stow the hay on our own, help from the Macs was welcome – and on top of that, there was always horseplay with them.

Getting the hay into the shed was one thing: getting it out for feed was another. The hay-knife was a simple yet practical tool for getting this done. It was composed of a giant unwieldy blade with a dobble handle on it. Using it, you could cut the needful quantity of hay from the store in the barn. This cutting out of the hay left a right-angled gorge, open on two sides; in which you could wonder at the sedimentary layers of hay. Moreover: the freshly cut hay smelt wonderful.

I never ceased cursing the hay knife, simply because I wasn't strong enough to apply it: the packed-down hay was just too dense to cut. That was Eugene's job, while I came completely into my own in dispensing feed to the cattle, the cow and Charlie. As it was only a few steps from the barn to the stalls, I'd take up as much hay as possible with both arms and take it to the stalls, though with it pressed to my chest I couldn't quite see where I was going. The cattle knew that their 'waiter' was approaching with their meal, tugged at their chains in an agitated manner and almost put their necks out, looking back to catch the direction head-waiter Herbert was coming from, to fill the byres with hay. As the bullocks wouldn't usually make way, but stood with their rears in a dense mass, I had to give a good roar: "Get around, will ye". As it had to do with food, the animals understood very well and immediately freed a small gangway between them. Roaring out these loud commands was great fun to me: I could shout as loud as I liked, and the cattle obeyed my commands.

On top of that, it was usually nice and snug in the cow-stall, so that I often lingered a while after bringing the fodder and watched the cattle eat. As well as that, being with the animals was always a refreshing experience, at least when they were standing tied up in their stalls and I could scratch and pet their heads and in return they'd lick the back of my hand with their rough tongues.

The hay knife

I was particularly fond of the suckers: we raised two of them in my time. The calf was taken away from its mother immediately it was born, brought to the 'old house', and put in the calf-stall surrounded by low concrete walls, which I described earlier on. There it would be fed from a bucket half full of milk: which was done by putting one or more fingers in the calf's mouth for it to suck and then dipping your hand along with the calf's mouth into the bucket, whereupon the calf would go on sucking ardently, wildly butting forward all the while. I seem to remember writing home to my parents and informing them that I was now up and running as a mother-cow.

Harvesting the oats was much the same as saving the hay. We didn't grow other kinds of corn so only Black Jack's corn had to be brought in, which again meant riding high on the cart and was great fun.

The sheaves of oats weren't taken into the barn, but were built up into a big stack in the garden. Threshing was done as it was needed with a flail or the sheafs would simply be beaten on a big stone.

Technology made its appearance in my second year: young farmers from our district clubbed together to buy a tractor with a threshing machine and hired themselves out in the district for the threshing. And how we gaped when they came to us. Above all there was the brand-new tractor, a gleaming, blue-laquered 'Fordson Major', which had the threshing machine hitched on. Up into the garden it came; transmission belts were put on, and off it went. Neighbours, who'd come round for the occasion, were sitting and standing about. They were amazed at the speed with which our stack got smaller and smaller. Granny appeared with several bottles of Guinness and a bottle of whiskey, and our first machine threshing became a mini-festival.

Threshing with the flail

129

35

Trips To Murneen And Belcarra

Mae and Eugene soon made me familiar with our neighbourhood. Our first "journey" took us to the village of Murneen, some four/five kilometres away, which was where their brother Simon had married into – and had already founded a grand family of five children: I got on mighty well with Mary, Pat, John, Claire, and Raymond from the word go, and it was Claire who kept up my family link with the Nally Family after my branch had either emigrated or died. Simon and his wife Nancy ran a country corner shop as well as their farm; and Simon also did some rural trading in a small way, collecting the eggs from locals in his mobile shop and stocking a small assortment of wares in daily use. His vehicle – a rectangular shaped cart with a canvas roof was drawn by a mare. It was as well-known as a spotted dog, and was part of the countryside. "Simon's coming", people would say as soon as they heard the characteristic knocking of his axle in the distance.

The shop itself was a first-rate general store: from pitch-forks to giant brooms, from barrels of paraffin to rubber-boots, from sacks of wheat-flour to shoe-polish, not forgetting tobacco and cigarettes – it was all there. For me the big tea-chests conveyed a great spirit of adventure: made of plywood, with aluminium strips nailed in all around the edges, they carried the mysterious markings of exotic Indian cities. When their lids were lifted with a crow-bar and the parchment-like paper was turned back, the scent of tea would overwhelm all the other smells in the shop for a while. To cap it all, there were always people in Simon's Shop. Quite apart from shopping, all sorts of other business would be done there, right up to match-making. The place was interesting at any time of day, and Simon's Shop could hold its own with Reuters as a news agency at any time.

We had a similar country shop in Ballinlough. It belonged to Pat and Delia Staid, brother and sister, and was in the dip near the cross-roads. They were the Uncle and Aunt of my friend, Jack Staid. Pat and Delia's shop was well-known around the Ballinlough area, not so much for its modest selection of goods but for its radio. The men and boys of the whole district would come and participate in the football on a Sunday – then Pat and Delia had a full house. But more of that later.

Often I'd have to run across the fields to Staids' when Eugene gave me the errand of getting him some cigarettes from Pat's. Usually that would mean getting a couple of loose Wild Woodbines or Players: it would have been too dear to buy a box. Somewhere in Martin Nevin's field there must still be a thru'penny bit which I lost while running diagonally across it.

Pat's barn at Christmas-time left a more macabre, but enduring, impression. It was filled with hundreds of stone-dead turkeys: long rows of them, strung up by their feet from the shed roof and with their heads hanging down. Pat would buy them from the farms round about and export them to the States at Christmas. At any rate, that is what Pat and Delia told me again and again: they insisted that Mayo turkeys were the best known and most sought over there.

Shortly after that first visit to Murneen, I was sent off one day in the ass-cart to get something or other. Just a few metres before Simon's Shop, the Claremorris/Sligo railway line crossed the country road. Irish railway crossing barriers used to be great wooden gates, which were swung across the road if a train was coming. If no train was expected, the gates were swung back and blocked the lines. When I arrived with my donkey, the road was closed and several people were waiting, chatting with level crossing keeper McDonald. I hadn't learned Irish donkey-commands yet, so I availed of the old German coachman's command, "Brrrrrr", to stop him. The Irish looked at me with complete amazement, breaking into roaring laughter: "he's resourceful!", shouted one; another asked: "Are you cold in this fine weather?" The ice was broken, and after that every time I'd meet McDonald he'd say, "Hello Brrrrrrr, how are ye?"

On a later spin to Murneen I had an encounter which flummoxed me and set me wondering. The boreen to Murneen went through Townalough, along the lonesome Bog Road, past our turf-bank and from there onto the Kiltimagh-Claremorris tar road. Not far beyond our turf-bank, the boreen bent sharply to the left. There, to the left and right of the road, five or six horse-drawn wagons were lined up – two- and four-wheeled – or rather houses on wheels. They were gaily painted all round, with semi-circular roofs and pretty decorated windows. Exotic-looking women in long bright dresses and big shawls sat at several open fires, with cooking pots set on them. There were men with big hats on their heads, and children were running about. To the front and rear of the wagons, shaggy, piebald horses were tethered and grazing. Washing was hanging out to dry on the thorny furze-bushes.

My first thought was: Red Indians; my initial feeling: this is uncanny. A little uneasy, I trotted past this exotic bivouac with my ass-cart, calling

Tinkers on the roadside

Hello! to the left and Hello! to the right and – my greeting was politely returned. Arriving in Murneen, they enlightened me: I'd come across Tinkers. Tinkers are Irish pot-menders; they're a travelling people with their own language, whose origins haven't been entirely clarified, even now. They certainly aren't Gypsies, Roma, or Sinti. The roots of the Tinkers are as old as those of the Celts themselves, the original inhabitants of the country.

They weren't well-regarded by the Irish, being simply ignored. So there was a little bit of racism amongst my Irish. Back then, I allowed myself to be infected by the prevailing much slighter bias, and every time I had to pass camping Tinkers in my ass-cart, I'd thrash my donkey into a gallop. Just get past quick. Tinkers had their own self-appointed resting places, away from the main roads, like this one near Townalough Village, and certainly they were never bothered at them. [62].

Meanwhile I'd got to know my little donkey better and come to know his idiosyncrasies. He was neither lazy nor malevolent, but had a head of his own, his pride, and an amount of intelligence: which is to say he was an Irish donkey. If I did him wrong, he'd let me know it, was well able to retaliate, sometimes maliciously snapping at my bottom. But if I was nice to him, he was to me, and obediently followed every command. On top of that, in the early days he knew his way around better than I did. Once we'd set off for Murneen and had passed Crukaun Doite without me steering him into the turn-off, he needed no further guidance from the reins and could find his way there without further direction. At any rate, the two of us undertook some fine journeys.

Now and again I'd have to go to Balla with two or three sacks of oats: there was a little motor-mill at the far end of the town. It was a crushing-mill which turned the grain into oatmeal for feed. In fine weather these journeys were pure pleasure, particularly as they'd often be linked with skiving off school. But in wet and stormy weather they were a torment. I'd sit on my ass-cart, huddled up in old sacks, which were supposed to protect me against the rain, cold and – on occasion – storm-force winds.

But, once I got to the mill, I really came into my own: the mill-engine was a static Deutz diesel motor 'Made in Germany', (in Cologne to be accurate). And I knew the Deutz Motor Company, on the Deutz-Mülheim road in Cologne well: I used to pass it in the tram and out on walks with Father. On top of that, Opa Johann once worked there as a cast-dresser and told us a lot about the place. So I repeatedly had to describe the situation of the motor-works on the banks of the Rhine to the mill-hand, and explain the ins and outs of the kind of work Opa did there . . again, and again, and again. Now and then the lad would go into the pub next door and come back with a couple of old men: "Herbert, tell us . . . ." – and I'd have to start my stories all over again. If I tried to do what nearly all Irish story-tellers

Claremorris, Main Street in older times

do, make things up or embellish the tale from imagination, they'd jump on me. "Hey, that can't be right, you told it differently before". But I was always glad to tell them the stories, particularly as they didn't ask me to sing.

I was given a further mark of confidence, one of which I was rightly proud: I was to bring our three fattened pigs to Claremorris Bacon Factory. Mae had by this time already emigrated to America, and only Granny, Eugene and me were left on the farm. Eugene had other work he had to do, so he entrusted the three pigs to me and, more important, the bringing home safely of the abbatoir weight-card, on which payment depended. Early one morning, with Jack Staid's brother, Jim, helping, the three pigs were heaved into the ass-cart, now fitted out with the slatted sides we used for shifting turf. Coachman Herbert took his place and off we went. The journey took us past Facefield to Brize Castle, and then onto the tar road to Claremorris – a good 8 kilometres in each direction. I stood proudly in the midst of our three grunting, squealing pigs; my donkeen trotting indefatigably and good-temperedly into the glorious day; friends and strangers were greeted; and the drivers of the motor-cars, which passed me every quarter-hour at most, would salute me with their horns.

At Claremorris we made for the far end of the town, out onto the road towards the Bishopric of Tuam, and then we'd arrived. Several carts were assembled and, as we stood waiting, the drivers looked over each other's pigs – including mine – with an expert eye. I was quite unconcerned and played my part. The weighing itself I can no longer recall, only the long

My wife Karin looking at the Plains of Mayo. In the background Croagh Patrick.

Taking a break in the "Settlement in the mist"

paper strip, recording the weights and other data, which I carefully put into an envelope brought for the purpose and stashed between my vest and shirt. On the way home I'd feel for it again and again, to reassure myself it was still there. But such caution didn't prevent me parking donkey and cart in Claremorris, first at Byrne's Shop to buy a *tosheen* (a twist of paper) of toffees, and then at the pub on the corner of Main Street and Convent Road for a glass of ginger-ale. I enjoyed the marvellous feeling of being able to reach into my pants pocket and bring out a handful of coins – pence, half-pence, three- and six-penny bits, and even a shilling – to pay my "tab". The decor of the pub – I think it was Merricks Corner Pub then – was fantastic: lots of old photographs on the walls; and a long bar. A particular source of fascination was the long colourful row of whiskey bottles, standing on their heads, each with a dispensing mechanism: the barman only had to push it up with a glass to release the contents. Of course I was no stranger to the pub. After the Claremorris Cattle Fair Eugene would often take me with him when he went in for a drink. While he had his Pint, I'd be quite content with my glass of ginger ale or lemonade.

The longest journey I ever undertook with donkey and cart was to Belcarra, where Eugene and Mae's brother, Martin, had married into a farm. The journey took me through Balla and out onto the Castlebar Road into flat countryside, called The Plains of Mayo. This is entered through a long incline up a mountain – a kind of Drumlin. From the top of it there's a fine view across the plain right up to Croagh Patrick. [63]

Continuing on to Belcarra, I passed numerous farm-houses thatched with straw, which were common then. (Since then the furious Irish drive for modernisation has led to the virtual disappearance of these absolutely beautiful thatched cottages: they're a rarity in present-day Ireland. But Martin lives in one of them, which he has kept in absolutely perfect order.)

Martin was known far and wide for his magnificent swearing, and his first question to me was to ask for strong German swear-words, which I was able to supply him with. The German version of *Pog mo hón* was conveyed to him, as were *Drecksack* (dirty sack), *Blötschkopp* (block-head), and *Hurensohn* (son of a whore). Unfortunately Martin failed to remember this German vocabulary and, when I looked in on him in 1955, he was swearing in Irish/English again.

There was a forge at the entry to Belcarra, where I stopped to watch, as I'd never seen horses shoed before. Charlie didn't wear horse-shoes, nor did our donkey: they would have cost too much.

I have fond memories of the country roads, particularly the narrow Boreens. All the village or country roads around Ballinlough, apart from Facefield, were boreens: small and narrow. Driving along them in the Spring was a colourful delight: the ditches glowed yellow with thorny furze and red with wild fuschia, while the strip along the middle beamed a rich green contrast. But the boreens fed the ear as well as the eye. Birds of every

A Ballinlough Boreen today. The lovely and characteristic ditches to the left and right are gone, replaced by wire fences.

musical kind sang and rejoiced in the hedges and bushes down the edges; and those on foot or cycling could often hear the soothing murmur of water flowing along drainage ditches, mostly running alongside.

But that is not to say that our country roads or boreens were left untended. I remember some of the older lads undertook road-works for the County Council every Winter. 'Doing road works for the County Council' put a shilling in the pocket for many a lad. Jack's brother, Jim Staid, as I recall, did road works for several weeks, using the horse (Staids had a mare) cart. Holes were filled in, drainage ditches cleared and unruly growth was cut back. These days even the smallest boreen is asphalted, though often just a thin layer is applied. That doesn't quite take away its peculiar charm, but most boreens aren't what they once were. In my time there were no nasty machines running along the edge of the road, cutting away everything Mother Nature provides to make travelling a joy. But of course in those days an overhanging branch wasn't a danger to traffic, as it is today.

The Brize Battle

As Granny Nally was no longer good on her feet, it was incumbent on me to bring her to Mass in Facefield by carriage. We owned an elegant, two-wheeled Pony Trap (also called Tub Cart), which had solid rubber tyres.

But, hitched to our donkey, it had several disadvantages. For one, I couldn't keep up a smart pace: the donkey wasn't fast enough for that. And, for another – and this was the more vexing – the donkey was smaller than an Irish pony, meaning that my vehicle listed downwards at the front in a loathsome way. I would always feel ashamed driving this crooked, mis-hitched vehicle into Facefield. Granny knew this and would try to console me: "Don't mind, Herbert. It's for a good cause. After all, we're driving to Our Lord."

One Sunday there was a spectacular happening: People from Brize Village used to take a short-cut to get to Church in Facefield – one which brought them through two fields belonging to the McEveneys – fields they'd sown with oats. The

Pony trap

136

Brize people tramped their Mass-path through the crop. The Macs, as the McEveneys were known by one and all, several times asked the Brizers not to do this: naturally they were ignored. On this particular Sunday the McEveney brothers – Jim, Mike, and Paddy – crept out of Church before the end of Mass and took up defensive positions behind a ditch near one of their gates. When several Brizers turned up, there was a mighty argument, which degenerated into a scrap such as would have been sheer joy to the Celtic ancestors of our Macs.

At first the rest of the Church-goers had no idea of the martial turmoil going on nearby. They'd gathered in front of the Church for their customary Grand Palaver. It was only after a Brizer messenger came running up, yelling long before he'd got near: "The Macs are fighting us" – that the crowd moved to the scene of the action. Us youngsters rushed over, of course. And what a sight! As in the times of the Celtic King *Conn Ceadchadhach* (Conn of the 1000 Battles), they weren't just fighting standing upright: in some cases the fallen were still fighting on in the melee. Jim McEveney's fiery red head appeared now and again above the heap, only to be immediately re-despatched down to the lower realm of the battle-arena by a punch. His brother Paddy came crawling out of the ruck, got up and made a flying tackle back into the fight – which was starting to go against the Ballinlough men: six or seven Brizers against three Macs, there was no future in that.

Meanwhile the Brizer war-messenger brought his martial intelligence to our priest, Father Lowry, appealing to our man of God for a quick intervention and sorting out. But the chain-smoking Father Lowry used to allow himself a little break after his onerous religious duties, and was enjoying the Wild Woodbine cigarette he'd just lit, his third. He finished it before acting.

We could hear the priest's wheezing lungs before we actually saw the man of God, wearing his soutane. But then our courageous priest, bellowing like we'd never heard before, launched himself between the fists flailing like windmills. By sheer luck no stray punch landed on him and, by force of his authority, he was able to separate the warring parties. But they only reluctantly departed the field of battle, sporting bloody noses, swellings on their faces, and their Sunday best torn ragged.

This thrilling intermezzo had consequences for me as well. Because we in the Ballinlough Gang went on to evaluate events, and to consider whether we shouldn't give our Brizer class-mates a sound thrashing on Monday as a mark of solidarity with the Macs, Granny drove herself home alone. When I belatedly arrived, a picture was painted to me of all that might have happened if our donkey had taken one of his moods and bolted – along with Granny and the trap. For the first time there was some discord between us, yet it soon evaporated. But it was a lesson to me.

36

Adventure Fair Day

The grandest and most thrilling variations to the everyday routine of farm life were the Cattle Fairs or Fair Days, not just because the farmers could look forward to a profit when selling their cattle, but also because they were a community experience. Fair Days were always social events with the feel of a popular festival. Our nearest Cattle Mart was in Balla and, if I recall rightly, it was held four times a year: July, August, September, and October.

All along both sides of Balla Main Street, from the Church up to the Crushing Mill, there'd be lined up facing the pavement: bullocks, heifers, calves, and cows – with horses and donkeys interspersed here and there – along with sheep and young pigs (*bonhams*) penned up in donkey carts.

The animal droppings would have made the street a slippery irridiscent green. Cheap Jack would have set up his stall, where you could buy practically anything – from galvanised buckets to a Sunday suit – "cheap". Thimble-riggers of one kind or other would be standing in house-doorways or on the corners, and there'd also be some wheels of fortune turning.

Potential buyers of the fine array of livestock on offer – some of them down-right crooks acting for the Dublin slaughter-houses or for exporters – would stroll along the line of cattle-arses, apparently bored, but registering the position of the best bullocks with a fine sensibility.

And what a great show it was – more gripping and dramatic than many a theatre play – when it came to the point: making the bargain. Now buyer and seller would start shouting at each other, as though they were about to come to blows; now there'd be flattery and courtship; then a vendor would turn away from an offer, apparently totally overwhelmed with disgust and having lost all interest. In his turn, the purchaser would walk away from the scene of the negotiations, spitting fire and brimstone over the audacity of the asking price – only to turn up again a quarter of an hour later to make a new bid.

When the encounter starts approaching the hot point of a deal, a crowd of spectators gathers, who not only watch and comment loudly, but often take a hand in the proceedings. During this phase, buyer and seller slap the flat of each other's hands with some force and recklessness. Hands are stretched out and pulled back at lightning speed; now and then slaps coincide with the simultaneous calling out of the sum demanded or offered. During this final phase, what's at issue is often "only" Half-a-Crown (two

Fair day in Balla (1955)

old shillings and six pence) – and it can go on and on. Once the vendor shakes hands and the bargain is sealed at last, the pound notes change hands. But then the seller gives the Half-Crown back to the buyer – the same coin over which they've just been haggling and delaying so hard and long – for luck, along with the animal! But naturally that didn't go for the Dublin buyers, or those from other big cities.

Eugene often took me to Fair Days in Balla, Claremorris or Kiltimagh, even if we had nothing to buy or sell, just for the pleasure of it, or to watch how the prices were going.

Naturally we also sold cattle. Once it was three, and another time before that it was four fine fat bullocks. These would be separated from the rest of the herd the evening before and driven into a small field near the house.

Spinning a yarn with Martin Nally of Belcara (left). He was to sell his ram at Balla fair, 1955.

Next morning we'd be up before first cock-crow.

After a full Irish breakfast – fried bacon, eggs, white pudding and black pudding, usually reserved for Sundays – it was out into the dawn.

My job was to guide the cattle and I had to stop the bullocks from breaking out to the front or turning off into by-ways and boreens which led the wrong way. I also had to stop them climbing over ditches to get to their fellows in the meadows behind.

Eugene was the backstop, who had to keep the mini-herd together and drive it on. All this was bound up with a lot of shouting, which got even louder when other farmers and their animals were turning into our road and their bullocks tried to get into our group. Swear-words such as I'd never heard before would be uttered, which Fr. Lowry would take pleasure in at next Confession.

I was kept busy non-stop: first blocking off some wrong side-road and then flitting forward to bar off the next wrong turn. It wasn't unusual for the agitated bullocks to drive me off the roadway into drainage ditches – and the water in these would always be at least ankle-deep. With soaking wet feet in soaking wet shoes, I'd often end up in a race when the cattle – who after all hadn't a clue about what was happening, as they were only driven to the cattle-mart once in their cattle-lives – got agitated for some reason and broke into a gallop. Then I'd have to overtake the leader to regain my blocking role. This would continue until we hit the tar road to Balla, when there'd be relative peace. Arriving in Balla, there'd be another lot of chaos, worse but much shorter, till we got our bullocks into place where we wanted.

The sale of the four cattle, probably at the 1947 October Fair in Balla, was the first time I took an active part in a Fair Day, and it brought a small "fortune" to the Nallys – and to me as well. Because our cattle were ready for slaughter, and so wouldn't be sold on to another farmer, Eugene made a successful deal with one of the crook Dublin buyers. Forward and cheeky as I then was, I'd now and again add my bit of mustard to Making the Bargain and caught the attention of the Dub. "Say, know-all, where are you from?", the Dublin crook asked. "From Germany!" I replied with dignity, puffing my chest out proudly, and Eugene laughed up his sleeve. After more chat the Dub asked me if I'd mind driving the four bullocks up to the railway station. As Eugene had no objection, I trotted up with them. Balla Railway Station lay at the edge of the town. It had a loading ramp, with several iron cattle-pens set into it. One of these had been rented by the crook and had his number on it. With the help of a grown-up knocking about the station, I got the four cattle into the pen and went off to join Eugene in the local. The Dub found me there, asked if it had all worked out and – put his hand in his trouser-pocket and picked a Half-Crown piece out of a handful of change, which he gave me with the words, "Well done". I was over the moon: a Half-Crown, that was a fortune to a youngster like me in those days! And – I swore by God and all his angels that I'd never call a crook from Dublin a crook again.

Eugene sold his four bullocks for £18 Pounds apiece. As I'd been involved, I now knew that the Nallys had a "fortune" of at least £72 at their disposal. Whether the Nallys were rich or poor or in-between I never did find out. They never talked about money – even to me, who was one of the family. And that's how it is: the Irish person won't talk about his money, even if the Dear Lord threatens him with Purgatory. And another fact: there are two things a right-thinking Irish person hates like the plague: the devil and the taxes!

That the Irish – at least any that I've had to do with – were mean, I can flatly contradict, even though they had Celtic blood, like the Scots who are legendary for their meanness. Certainly the Irish farmers of those days would turn every Penny over twice before spending it, but that's because they'd have to work so hard for their money and to survive in the Ireland of the late forties,. Manufactured goods were very much over-valued compared to agricultural produce in those days – and the farmers got a very poor return on this as well.

I lacked for nothing at the Nallys. I was clothed just as all my friends were by their parents. I had my good suit, naturally with short pants. Me and my friends called these Sunday suits our "Sunday-going-to-Mass-suits" because they were only worn for going to Church. Likewise the "Sunday-going-to-Mass-shoes". I had an ongoing bone of contention with the Nallys over shoes. My friend Jack had "clogs" for the Winter – and he wasn't the only one. These were good-value footwear with leather uppers and a thick wooden sole, with a piece of wire nailed in all around the edge. Jack was able to use them to skate on the ice of the lake, just like skates, and

141

he could slide on them for metres. I was simply hopeless with my leather shoes

But, quite apart from that, the clogs particularly appealed to me, especially as nearly all my friends wore them. My wishes were categorically refused by the Nallys, and all my begging and entreating didn't help. They explained that these cheap things – the clogs were inexpensively bought from Cheap Jack on Fair Days – are not for you. You'll wear leather shoes, end of story! The Nallys weren't going to have it said that their German urchin had to run around in clogs. And me? I could have howled over remaining clogless for the whole of my Irish life.

As opposed to our smart Sunday best, our everyday attire had a rakish look. Anything was worn, even handed-down clothes. There was no such thing as work-clothes. There's a photo of me wearing my everyday outfit – with one addition. As there'd been a prior announcement about a school-photograph, Granny quickly put a tie around my neck, as was proper. But I must have "forgotten" my legs, particularly to wash my knees – as can be seen on the photo. *(Page 104)* To put on our Sunday-best for the occasion: that simply didn't occur to any of us – vain, we weren't.

By this time – this would have been coming up to the Winter of 1947-48 – I was already thoroughly integrated into my Nally Family, and into my immediate Irish environment in Ballinlough and beyond. I was no longer anything out of the ordinary, either for my Ballinlough Gang, or at school. I was hardly ever asked about Germany, and then mainly by older people. Only one of my neighbours – I think it was old Murphy up the road, with whom I had a yarn now and again, questioned me about Germany regularly. His special interest was the German military and particularly Rommel's tanks. And he always greeted me in the same way: "How are ye Herbert! When do we go up to the North and beat the British?"

My friends had accepted me and treated me in an exceptionally comradely way: I was accepted as one of them. My mother-tongue, German, was melting way, the more so since – apart from letters from home – I never saw it written, let alone heard a single word of German. Yet I must have anticipated the work of the later Goethe Institute [64] for, when I met up with my old school-friends after near-enough 40 years, several of them surprised me by repeating to perfection German phrases which I'd once taught them. Jack, for instance, said: *"Guten Tag, mein Herr, wie geht es Ihnen?"* (Good day, sir, how are you doing?); and Seamus Gannon: *"Dies ist ein Füllfederhalter"* (This is a fountain-pen) Even my old teacher, Malachy Garvey, now 90 years old, could still remember: *"Dies ist einKater"* (This is a Tom-cat).

And my general behaviour didn't stand out any more, as I'd internalised customs and usages, and the modes of expression of everyday life. If I was in Balla or Claremorris for shopping or something, I'd still be asked about my accent, which sounded a bit German. But even this disappeared in time.

The Irish Red Cross, which after all was responsible for me, directed that I should be presented to a lawyer in Balla every six months to be asked about my well-being. This was done and, as I had nothing to complain about, we'd discuss this and that in private, just the two of us. I'd chat to the good man for half an hour, amusingly I hope; and on account of that he probably got a juicy honorarium from the Red Cross while, in turn, I'd get from him a magnificently bulging bag of toffees. No doubt about it, I was glad to call on him.

At the Nallys I'd grown into my role of youngest "son" and "brother", and was treated as such. I had my daily tasks, most of which I liked doing and a few of which less so. One of these was fetching water from the spring, really a field-well. This was actually a round hole, about one to one-and-a-half metres deep, encircled by a dry-stone wall made of field-stones as a surround - and finish. We couldn't call any of the field-wells our own, and we also used mostly neighbour Staid's well or the Nevins' on occasion.

I had to trot the 300 metres to the Well and carry back a ten-litre bucket in each hand, not exactly effortless. Sometimes I'd use the Nevins' Well, which meant balancing my way over a ditch, which sometimes went amiss.

But the water was crystal clear and absolutely pure – even though frogs sported in it, and waterboatmen and other kinds of wildlife lived in it.

On one occasion there was a row with Eugene over the water-fetching. He took me to task because all the buckets were empty. But I'd reached my reading years, had just managed to snap up a book somewhere, and my mind was absorbed in the adventure. "I won't tell you again", says Eugene, already very angry. "Yes, yes, right away", I reply – and so it went on.

But then Eugene blows a gasket. He jumps up, wanting to give me my first ever wallop. But I'm gone in a flash, the book thrown aside: out of the door, through the little front garden, over the road past the Turf Reek, into the field and – Eugene right behind me. I make it to the first ditch gate, Eugene hot on my heels, incandescent with rage and constantly trying to grab me. Exhausted I let myself fall – and Eugene lands beside me on the grass. We look at each other – and both start roaring with laughter simultaneously.

All the rage of my "big brother" had evaporated, and my fear as well. Arm in arm we walk back to the house, where Granny's been anxiously watching the chase. Now she comes towards us, satisfied. Granny didn't like strife.

37

My Irish Granny

As for my Irish Granny: if only every child could have such a loving Oma. Granny was a gentle woman: soft-spoken, sweet and tender. Never a cross word from her, never a cross look. Granny always dressed in black: full black skirt; black apron, tied at the back with a big bow; black blouse, plain; black jacket; black coat. Grandpa Nally died the year before I came. But Granny wasn't just wearing black in grief: it was a sort of traditional wear for older ladies. It certainly wasn't peasant-wear – for there never were any in Ireland. The British had seen to that in their colonial days. They would only tolerate the existence of poor tenants, not peasants with land and property rights.

Without ever making any arrangements, or giving lectures to Mae and Eugene about their work, Granny determined home-life, just by being there.

Before bed-time, when she'd kneel down in front of her chair and get out her rosary, then we'd also kneel in front of our chairs, our arms propped up, and join in the prayers: "Our Father, who art in Heaven..., Hail Mary, Mother of Mercy..., Hail Mary, full of Grace..."

Naturally Granny had an attentive listener in me, particularly as she had an abundance of Irish legends and myths. She had the power of telling stories about the Fairies, the elves who lived in the bushes at Cruckaun Doite, in such a true-to-life and realistic way that we used to walk past it very fast on the way to and from school. If you found the right spot down on Tawny Lake, the Fairies would give you a sight of *Tir na nOg* (Land of Eternal

My Irish Granny with her sons Simon, Eugene, Tom and Simon's children, John, Pat, Claire, Raymond, Mary (from the left)

Youth). But however often I searched its shores, I was never granted that look at *Tir na nOg*.

"Of course", says Granny, "the Fairies only show themselves at harvest-time, on bright moonlit nights. You'll have to wait a bit longer."

Granny told me about the Grogochs who, on account of their diligence, reminded me of the Cologne *Heinzelmännchen* (Brownies, Little People), my Cologne Oma Gertrud often told stories about. And naturally Granny had tales about the Leprechaun, the shoemaker who's always drunk – and is nowadays to be got in the tattier Irish Souvenir Shops, wearing plush clothes of glaring green. Pooka, the ghost, was feared. If he looked at the Farm, the hens wouldn't lay any more and the cows would fall dry. And there was Dullahan, the headless horseman, who rides the Bog for ever and a day. If the Fir Darig, the red-clothed dwarf, should come by, says Granny, I ought to let him into the house. He'll only sit at the fire, to warm himself up. But Granny was less eager to tell me about the Banshee, the white woman, who always shows herself to people howling and combing her hair. But anyone who sees the Banshee must die: she is the harbinger of death. (Joesie Cunningham's husband, who trained a boxing team somewhere in Dublin, was on the bridge crossing the Grand Canal on his way home, when he suddenly called to his companion, that he could see the Banshee sitting down below, on the pier of the bridge. That very same night he died of a heart-attack.)

Naturally I myself have truly and honestly seen the Irish ghosts and Fairies, and heard them too.

One of our heifers was pregnant and the birth of the calf was imminent. As it was Summer, and the cow mother-to-be was grazing on our cut-away bog with the other cattle, Eugene didn't want to bring her back to the stable. So he suggested that I should stand guard out there overnight. I wasn't exactly happy about that idea, as I was in a blue funk about standing a night-watch on my own, and in a place that was full of ghosts on top of that. But my friend Jack said he was willing to stand guard with me. Next to the turf-moor was a small sugar-loaf-shaped rise called Croagh Mór, from which we could overlook the whole bog in the bright moonlight of this Summer's night, particularly as moonlight in Mayo is almost as bright as daylight.

In short: Jack and I are sitting up there by a tiny fire and are telling each other about this and that when suddenly we hear the dull clatter of the hooves of countless horses. We jump up and look towards the Bog and – see nothing but our cattle, lazily lying around. We look again, and yet again, the galloping of a herd of horses in our ears – but we can see no horses. We look at each other, our faces white. The herd gallops past and everything goes quiet again. But we're both certain: that was the headless Dullahan with his troops.

Croagh Mòr

The next day our pregnant heifer is confined and our excitedly-told story is noted in silence. *(This experience never went out of my head and in 1955, I revisited Ireland for the first time, meanwhile having gained some knowledge of physical phenomena. I refused to be deprived of a return to Croagh Mór and a stroll over our old bog. At the far side, a long way away, were the pastures of a farmer who'd always raised horses. That seemed to point at an explanation. On the night in question, this farmer's herd of horses started moving, for whatever reason, and galloped about. The lower reaches of the bog are soaking wet, and it's possible that the moor floats on a bubble. This took up the clatter of horses' hooves and transmitted the sound to the foot of Croagh Mór. As a result we could hear without seeing anything.)*

Again a moonlit Summer's night in Mayo: so bright that you could read a newspaper, should such a thing be to hand. We had visitors in our house, local farmers who'd come over sometimes to chat: the Macs were there; also Navvy Staid and my friend Jack, who'd come with his father. Towards midnight the young men ran out of cigarettes – the older ones only smoked pipes – and the two of us were given the errand of going down to Pat Staid's shop to buy a few.

In the moonlight the trees, bushes and ditches threw long, confusing shadows – particularly the thorny furze growing on the ditches – and the countryside lay before us as though bathed in silver. This was Mayo at its best! On the way home, just before Anthony Regan's Farm, we saw them: the Fairies. They were dancing on the ditches, swaying weightlessly to and fro in the moonlight, in long almost transparent garments. A minute or two and they were gone. Our excited report was smiled at at home. But Jack and I knew: we'd seen them!

By the way: Visiting Houses ('Rambling Houses' in North Cork) were homes where people came visiting practically every night. At one time there were several such houses in Ballinlough as well. But in my time Pat Staid's in the dip had become the main one. He ran a general shop in his house with his sister, somewhat comparable to Simon Nally's in Murneen.

Pat and Delia Staid, both unmarried, were the only ones to have a wireless, which is why all our neighbours, and Eugene as well, ended up visiting only there. This meant that the practice of visiting the other houses was almost completely lost.

On top of everything else, my Irish Granny was a reliable weather forecaster and knew a rule for every natural phenomenon: if the curlew flies very low, calling loudly, then there'll be snow. If Christmas is green, the cemetary will fill. Red sky at night, shepherd's delight; red sky in the morning, shepherd's warning. The Dutchman's Trousers, which Granny set great store on, enables me even today to make a fairly accurate forecast of our Continental weather when the sky is overcast. If a tiny blue hole appears in the clouds – the Dutchman's Trousers – the weather will turn sunny.

Another thing: our house in Ballinlough occupied a privileged position, one that would be the envy of 95 per cent of the Catholic Irish: on a clear day we could see right across to towering Croagh Patrick, just 40 kilometres away on the Atlantic Coast, near Westport. This is Ireland's Holy Mountain, on which St. Patrick is said to have spent several weeks, just praying and performing miracles. It's from there that he's said to have driven all the snakes out of Ireland – and it's a fact that there aren't any in the country.

Croagh Patrick, the Reek as we called it, was our weather-station. If it was wreathed in cloud, the weather would improve but if it, in all its beauty, seemed tangibly near, then rain was coming. But I soon discovered: cloudy or fine, rain was always about.

Granny lived according to the usages of her youth in the Ireland at the close of the 19th century. If she went to bed before us, her last words to us would be: "mind the fire". The turf fire in the fireplace must never go out. One or two sods of turf would be put on the red coals, and then covered with ash so that there'd still be glowing embers in the morning, which could be got going to make the daytime fire.

But this would be difficult if it was stormy and there was driving rain, which might come into the chimney, trickling down the sides. On top of that, the chimneys were badly sooted up, and in those conditions soods (chunks of sodden soot) would come whistling down into the hearth – which always gave me a deadly fright! And, apropos, there's a fine weather adage in rhyme: "When the soods come down and the Spaniel sleeps and the spider from the cobweb creeps" – then the weather will be really miserable.

Every hearth had a "Heart Stone" at its centre. On moving into a new house, the Heart Stone would be brought along and built into the hearth. When the Nallys moved from their Old House into their newly-built one, the Heart Stone was left behind, because the hearth was going to be needed

The Hearth (painting by Mary McSweeney)

Notice the churn, front left

for cooking the pig-swill. Whenever I'd make a fire there, I'd first have to sweep all the ash from the Heart Stone and kindle the fire on clean stone. At the same time I'd have to ask the pardon of the Heart Stone for failing to keep the fire going in his fireplace. "Clean the stone!" Granny always reminded me.

Churning was another of my tasks. Our barrel-churn was held in its housing by two pegs. And you'd have to keep turning it with a crank-handle until you could hear the ball of butter tumbling about in the barrel. It was then down to Granny to carefully salt the butter and spread it into a round wooden mould, which was then turned out. The final step was to press a cross into the butter.

One day a neighbour came in while I was churning. Granny immediately pushed me away from the churn and gave the neighbour the crank, and he had to go on turning it until the ball of butter could be heard. And, another thing, no one was allowed to light his pipe with a piece of glowing turf while the butter was being churned.

A painful separation was in prospect: Mae was emigrating to America. Mae was around 25–26 years old at this time. In the Ireland of those days there were only three alternatives: remain a spinster, marry a farmer, or emigrate. There wasn't any career-training for young countrywomen, and only a limited number of jobs in the cities.

Mae wanted to get out of the narrow agricultural way of life and try for a better future in the USA. I remember the tearful farewells and Granny's sadness: after all, her last remaining daughter in the house was leaving home parts.

Eugene and I brought Mae to Balla Railway Station, probably in Martin Nevin's car, and I still remember how, desolated, we watched the train pulling away. Now we were alone: Granny, Eugene and I. Mae left a gap: she was always joyful, wasn't afraid to help out in the fields, and she was also a big help to Granny in the work around the house.

I myself, though eleven years old and still a long way from puberty, adored Mae's beauty: her red hair and fascinating green eyes. And I wasn't the only one. The Macs, all three of them, paid court to her, and competed with each other to make a conquest, but were refused by Mae in a light-hearted, but not hurtful, way.

I was also to miss the Saturday nights when Mae and Eugene did themselves up and cycled off to a dance in one of the dance-halls in the vicinity. They'd often have to put many a kilometre behind them, for instance to Belcarra – where one of the nicest of the dance-halls still survives, albeit under a preservation order.

Mae mothered me, helped me with my school-work, 'operated' to take many a thorn out of my feet, and treated many a wound. Granny's competence was boils, bruises, and swellings.

*

One time, Eugene was giving me a ride on the cross-bar of his bicycle, when we passed a pasture where a young bull was seeing to a cow. Naturally I started watching them, greatly interested. But this made me forget my feet, and my left foot got caught between the fork and the spokes – which hacked off nearly half of the ball of my foot.

Eugene rushed me back to the house, where Mae poured hydrogen peroxide into the wound, where it foamed and bubbled up. I won't mention the pain. The piece of hanging flesh was pushed back home, brushed with iodene and tied up. Finished.

At that time hydrogen peroxide and iodene were the only all-round medicines deriving from the pharmaceutical industry to be found in Irish farmhouses. For the most part home remedies – above all Whiskey or Poiteen – were the substitute for the doctor. Poiteen is a 'black' devilish brew, distilled from corn or potatoes, and is strong enough to knock out the strongest bull. 'Black' poiteen was distilled everywhere, in hidden places on the bogs or in mountain ravines, by so-called Moonshiners – whom I've never seen, let alone spoken to. The Gardai were as hot about 'black' distillers and possession of poiteen as the devil is about Holy Water, and heavy penalties were a threat. And every Irish person angrily dismisses the imputation of being a 'black' distiller, as well as the suggestion that he may have one or more bottles of poiteen hidden in the house. At the same time, every Irish household had, and still has today, a bottle of poiteen tucked away somewhere. Experienced poiteen drinkers describe its effect as follows: "You think your brain's loose".

Whiskey or poiteen were the universal remedies for internal illnesses. The adage, "Whiskey makes you sick if you are well and Whiskey makes you well if you are sick", says it all.

Granny was inconsolable for a long time after Mae's emigration. She'd borne thirteen children in the Old House next door. There in the narrow confines of this straw-roofed Irish cottage, she'd lovingly raised these children if not in poverty, at least in the sparse circumstances of Irish rural life at the time. And, all the while she'd the inescapable prospect before her, that all her children would leave her and go far away, mainly overseas: all, except one, who'd inherit the farm. That's the position she'd now reached. Of all her children, only Eugene was left to her, living in the house of his parents.

Naturally her children came to visit. During my time there were two such visits from America. But they'd become Americanised Irish, dressed in a manner that seemed quite strange to us: the men wearing gaudy ties, but – they smelt nice!

Peggy, I remember very well: she found my interest in reading very good and sent me books from America.

One of Granny's sons had served in the US Army during the war, had fought hard against the German Wehrmacht during the Ardennes offensive, and later was one of those to occupy Cologne. When he was due to visit, a coloured picture of the Cologne chathedral, which had been sent to us by my parents and occupied pride of place in the "living room", was taken down. Whether the Ami was sour about the Germans I can no longer remember, but I was a real stinker because of my hidden chathedral and kept my distance from him.

There was huge fun when Joe came visiting from Dublin, or even Joe and Tom together.

They hung about with the other Ballinlough fellows of their own age, particularly with Jim Staid, the Macs and the Halligans, and spent the time getting up to mischief. The next day, either there'd be a donkey running wild through the village, several empty preserve-tins tied to his tail, or a neighbour was vainly searching for his ass-cart. The lads had taken it apart during the night, heaved it up onto the shed-roof and reassembled up there.

Joe was always motorised when he came, first with the English version of the German Ford Eifel, but then one day he appeared with a powerful, though well-used, American car, an Oldsmobile.

The whole Nally Family fitted into it and we made some lovely excursions to Castlebar and Westport and we visited the brothers in Murneen and Belcarra. When we drove up in this calash, it was as though Lords and Ladies had arrived.

38

A Sportsday With Consequences

"The Sports" were local events, entirely arranged by local effort in an uncomplicated way and were usually completely spontaneous. On that account they offered magnificent entertainment and drew people from far and wide. Whether news of such events spread by word of mouth in the Irish manner, or whether an advertisement was put in the paper, I can no longer remember: I imagine the first.

At any rate our Sports took place just off the road coming into Balla, not far from Black Jack's, in a field provided by a farmer. The word was there'd be Sports on Conway's Field on the Balla Road: everybody knew where it was and they all came along – on bicycles, on foot, with horse- or ass-carts, with carriages or traps, and even the occasional motor-car, the number of which could be counted on the fingers of one hand.

There'd be running and jumping races; something like shot-putting; and wild kicking of a ball through the district by randomly-assembled teams.

Tricky horse jumps were erected, built with sticks, strong branches, and one-time even with a medium-sized tree-trunk, then off they went. And it was the normal farm work-horses which were ridden in the competition,

The races of Ballinlough: Tom and Joe on a visit at home

Joe with his (small) car on a visit at home

often without a saddle. Since seeing the bravura with which these Irish riders kept themselves on the broad backs of these heavy nags without saddles, while galloping hard and doing emergency braking in front of jump-obstacles; and after observing how these nimble farm-lads pulled themselves up on to the horse again after centrifugal forces had catapulted them from their mounts on a turn – I'm sure that cossacks and cowboys are small beer beside these Irish farmboy-riders.

Semi-legal showmen would also come, working Three-Card-Tricks and Thimbles, and one of them even had a mobile Roulette-Table – at which only he, or his straw-man, would win.

The shooting-range consisted of a small gate of squared timber, with a square metal sheet hanging from the cross-beams. It had a small hole bored through it, scarcely bigger than a diabolo in diameter. If you shot with the pellet gun through it, a bell behind the hole would ring. If it tinkled, you got your Penny stake back, and another shot free. By coincidence my first shot went home and then they cried out: "Yes. Rommel, he can do it". I never really got rid of that crap Rommel image and was often called that, and am to this day.

In the midst of this really enjoyable entertainment I happened to notice someone being carried over to one of the few motor-cars in a rush, which then speeded away in Balla direction. A little while later someone comes up to me: "Hey, Herbert, that was Eugene. He collapsed, looked like a corpse. They're bringing him to the hospital in Castlebar." I'm standing there, as though struck by lightning. Eugene in hospital, how come? He didn't say there was anything wrong with him. Granny and me alone on the farm, what's to become of us?

Wise people prevented me from running straight off home to Granny. Best wait to see what happens. Those who took him to the hospital are bound to come back with some news. And they did too: burst appendix.

I seem to have withstood the full three weeks as a young husbandman without Eugene. Fortunately the misfortune befell us between Spring, Turf cutting and the beginning of harvest, and there was usually a bit of relief between these heavy periods. I succeeded in keeping Granny from doing all the jobs which she was now determined to do, except for the milking of the cow and the feeding of the feathered stock which she refused to yield. No animal gave up the ghost on me, the pigs continued to fatten, and I saw to the order and neatness of the yard as much as I was able. Well done, good man, came from all sides – and my chest ached with pride.

We also pursued sports in Ballinlough and, at least in the Summer, it completely filled Sunday afternoons. Down at the Halligans, on a small boggy green, we built a "high jump" out of willow-sticks. Naturally the height of the jump was decisive, but it was just as thrilling landing afterwards: our heels would leave dark skid-marks on the soft bog-ground and make deep holes. The same applied with the long jump. Celia Halligan was the only girl to join in, and she was no worse than us in any way, rather the opposite.

Football would also be played, particularly on the green near our house. We used hurling balls, or even a small sponge ball. I'd worked hard on Mae, to get her to send us a real leather football from America as soon as she got there – and she did! A parcel came from America, with a football – unfortunately it was for American Football: an Egg. Great disappointment: the Egg was hardly used.

An alternative offered itself when a pig was being slaughtered in the vicinity. We'd immediately appear, diffidently asking for the bladder, which was usually given to us. Naturally not in the Villages, where the local youngsters would be after it themselves. The pig's bladder was blown up, briefly let dry, and could be kicked. Unfortunately, the fun didn't last too long, before the bladder was spoiled.

The slaughtering of the pig itself was a really sorry business. A shed door was taken down, laid on two blocks, and strong neighbours were called together. Their combined strength was used to lay the pig on the door and tie it down. Simon Nally was the preferred butcher, called upon to do the slaughtering all over the place. Simon took his endlessly long knife, scratched a cross somewhere in the lower neck of the pathetically squealing beast, and then shoved his knife through it up to the hilt, straight into the heart. Just a few seconds and the pig was dead.

The rest followed in the usual way, except that there wasn't much processing done. The blood would be made into Black Pudding, and all the neighbours got a bit of the pig. The prized parts were the bacon and ham which, heavily salted, was part of the Full Breakfast.

A 'passive' game of football would be played down at Pat Staid's, if a game in the Irish championship was being played and broadcast over the radio. Then Pat and Delia Staid's cabin would be full to overflowing on account of their radio, and people sat on upturned buckets, turf-sacks, or even on the ground, and listened to the *Radio Eireann* broadcast. So thick were the fumes from the old men's pipes, that the contents of several bottles of Stout – as Guinness was usually called – were needed to soothe the roughness in their throats.

The pipe-tobacco smoked was usually Bulwarks plug tobacco, rectangular blocks of which were usually stowed away simply by being tucked into the trousers pocket. I was always fascinated watching the old farmers, as they cut small strips from the blocks, crumbled them in their palms and stuffed their pipes. The blade of Navvy Staid's pocket-knife, which he only used for cutting tobacco and castrating the *bonniveen* (or *bonhans* = young pigs = *ferkel* in German), looked like a Turkish crescent. The knife had to be razor-sharp and was constantly sharpened on a whetstone.

But one more word about trousers worn by the older men: particulary their pocets. These pockets were a wonder to behold, when you think of everything they held. An Irish farmer's trouser pocket could produce, apart from the plug tobacco and the pocket-knife: a long nail, a short nail, a screw, a piece of string, a metre of twine, loose matches, a little bit of wire and other bits and pieces.

At any rate, I can recall no 'technical' problem out in the fields, which couldn't be solved by some item out of Eugene's trouser pocket. And Eugene wore light modern corduroys, not pants like the old men. If I rightly recall these were tailored out of heavy, thick and tightly-woven woolen material, resembling felt. I used to imagine that after they were taken off they could simply be stood upright and wouldn't fall over. At any rate, that's the idea their stiffness put in my head! These extremely hard-wearing trousers, which easily withstood a heavy downpour of rain, were held up either with braces – or with a leather belt – usually up around the chest for these pants went almost up to the arm-pits. These Irish farmers' trousers remain an abiding fascination for me, so much so that I'm surprised that no Irish song-writer has ever written a Song of Praise to them. At least we Germans have a literary work, a novel, *The Trousers Of Herr von Bredow* (*Die Hosen des Herrn von Bredow,* by Willibald Alexis), which is about Prussian-German trousers – so we are ahead of the Irish on the clothing front.

In any case these Irish pants – along with heavy, often hobnailed, boots, or equally heavy Wellingtons, and an old jacket – were as I recall the every-day wear of the Irish farmer of mature years in the County of Mayo. A cap and a grandfather shirt completed the outfit. But when I met these older gentlemen on Sundays at Mass, now dressed in smart 'Sunday-going-to-Mass-suits', I'd often fail to recognise them, so much do 'clothes make man', as the old proverb goes.

I'd have to report the same about the ladies – if I'd taken much interest in the clothes they were wearing. But I was also amazed at the charm and grace of the ladies (and of the coleens likewise) in Church on Sundays: their beauty was hidden by the heavy day-to-day routine on the farms.

The young men for the most part smoked cigarettes, which were mostly bought singly, rarely a packet, which was too dear. There was a brand, "Wild Woodbines", the fags a little thicker than a piece of straw – but cheap on that account. "Sweet Afton" was another brand, indeed the only internationally known make to carry the first two lines of a beautiful poem, with an equally fine graphic reproduction of the Afton River: "Flow gently, sweet Afton among thy green braes, flow, gently, I'll sing thee a song on thy praise" (Robert Burns).

Other popular brands were "Gold Flake", and "Players Navy Cut" – the packet of which was finely illustrated with the head of a sailor and a lifebelt.

But back to Sport: In those days the chief reporter on Radio Eireann was much idolised by every Irishman. Undoubtedly he would have been elected President, if he'd stood. Michael O'Hehir was his name; and, for ninety minutes he described every, yes every, movement of ball and player, and commentated at a speed which would put any cattle-auctioneer in the shade. Yet every word was distinct and clear, so that the team gathered at Pat's could not only concretely visualise the game, but sometimes there'd be an accompanying kick by reflex action, making the upturned bucket under the backside of one of the listeners fly away. A half-sentence spoken by the reporter is still in my ear today: "but the referee blows his whistle and the ball goes over to..." Us youngsters so loved imitating O'Hehir's reports that we anticipated Karaoke by elevating them into competitions amongst ourselves. Thus we'd sometimes sit on the wall which partitioned the school playground, and outdo each other in imitating his reporting.

39

Brush With Irish Politics

My first contact with Irish politics was on account of a man who lived just beyond Pat and Delia Staid's house. I'd got a slight idea of politics one day when I was making one of my journeys to Balla in the ass-cart, turning on to the tar road, I found election slogans painted up. (That was in the Election of 1948, which was won by the Coalition.) I couldn't make any sense of them, as I couldn't understand the words. Eugene enlightened me and my interest was awakened.

In short: beyond Pat Staid's, set a little back from the road, there lived Bernard Commons, who was the Claremorris elected representative on Mayo County Council and was also elected to the Dail in 1945. Bernie Commons belonged to the small farmers' party, Clanna na Talmhan, which fought for land-reform, and particularly for vacant land from the landlord era to be divided out among the small farmers at affordable prices. And he campaigned using all sorts of means, legal and illegal. In March 1947, which is to say during my time, he spent a month in Sligo jail, on account of not abiding by pledges not to breach the peace and for making seditious speeches. In one of his Dail speeches he said that he'd broken the law in every shape and form and would continue to do so in his effort to get the people their rights: "I have driven cattle into fields which didn't belong to me, I have thrown down fence-enclosures which were to stop me doing that, and I'm not a bit ashamed of it." But it was his failure not to hold to his pledge to hold to the peace which was the crucial point.

This man, about whom I was hearing so much, appealed to me, particularly as he reminded me of what Mr. Cunningham had told to me in Dublin about the Irish rebels. One day, as I was idling about the fields with my friend Jack Staid, we had the idea of making a visit to Bernie Commons, the rebel. And he received us in a decidedly friendly way, made us a Cup of Tea – I think he was a bachelor at the time – and we had a palaver about this and that for well over an hour: a bit about Germany, but mainly everyday things.

40

Wild Rabbits And Lambs' Tails

Jack Staid would always be with me in these free-time activities: we were inseparable. In the Spring we often wandered about on Croagh Móre and the Old Bog, where we drove our cattle so that they could graze on the fresh greenery. The Old Bog was a paradise for all kinds of birds, but particularly for ground-breeders, whose nests we found. Jack had his, I mine, and we made bets about which young birds would fly the nest first.

One Sunday afternoon we came across one of our cattle, sunk into a bog-hole at the foot of a dug-out turf-bank. Only the head and back still showed, and the eyes of the beast reflected mortal dread. We rushed back into the village and, beginning down by the Halligans, ran through calling for help. The men came running immediately, armed with ropes: there was no hesitation. I am no longer sure exactly how and where the ropes were slung around the poor beast. At any rate they succeeded, with a lot of effort, in pulling the animal out.

Now and again our horse Charlie was also brought down to graze in the Old Bog, which is how I got my only Irish riding lessons, apart from those on our donkey which were more a torment than a pleasure because of his protruding backbone. Without a saddle, in order to get on the farm-horse I first had to position him alongside a small wall, from which I then swung myself onto his broad back, where I sat with wide-stretched legs, a bit like doing the splits. If the nag trotted in a leisurely way, I'd bounce about up there and only my firm hold on his mane saved me from falling off. Only once did I impel Charlie into a restrained gallop which, however, I survived with bravura. However, when I had to bring Charlie back from the Old Bog the next day, in the absence of the wall, I had to lead him back by his rein!

One day an ancient delivery-cart turned up in Ballinlough, pitching about and rattling. It was covered with a tarpaulin and, as would-be competition for Simon Nally, was ignored – at least by the Nallys. But when the trader announced that he was also in the market for rabbits (for their fur), and that he paid, I think, Three Pence per mature specimen, there was no restraining Jack, who dug out old iron spring-traps, originally got for rats and probably foxes.

We also had some lying around on the farm. Jack showed me how to handle the traps, digging them in at the burrow exit and carefully disguising them. My catching area was mainly in Martin Nevin's field down in the low ground where a slope fell away from the ditch, an ideal situation for wild rabbits. After that, setting the traps was one of my spare time activities and, early in the morning, before setting off for school, I'd run to the ditches, to check the traps and bring home my bag.

This way of catching rabbits was really brutal and painful, because the poor creature was caught in the trap alive. Sometimes there'd only be a paw in the trap, the rest of the rabbit gone. It had either torn itself from its leg or the fox had got there before me. The numbers caught were satisfactory. If four rabbits were sometimes ready for collection in a week, and the dealer paid three pence apiece in single coins or Three-Penny-Bits, a Shilling (equal to twelve pence) was amassed. A Shilling a week was a princely income for a youngster in those days.

Jack also had a ferret with which we often went hunting. While the animal disappeared into the rabbit-hole like a flash of lightning, I'd stand ready with a sack at the other side of the ditch, at the presumed second exit of the burrow. It wasn't rare for the startled rabbit, rushing to make its escape from the hissing ferret, to plop straight into the sack.

Once lambing was over, then the "Spring Lambs" had their tails cropped. These lambs' tails were our booty. Singed and grilled over a fire, they were delicious to gnaw at, but there wasn't much flesh on them of course.

I can't remember the main festivals – Christmas, Easter or even St. Patrick's Day – but make up for it with Halloween (Snap-Apple Night). Although it was an ancient Celtic Feast, the grown-ups didn't make a lot of fuss about Halloween. I can't recall that anyone ran about wearing masks, grotesque faces, and exotic clothing. We children went round from house to house, and each house had a fine big apple hanging from the ceiling on a thread. And a bowl full of water stood ready with a coin on the bottom: a Penny, a Three-Penny-Bit or even sometimes a Six Pence Piece. If, your hands crossed behind your back, you managed to bite into the apple, you got a Penny. And if you were able to "dip" into the bowl of water and get the coin out with your mouth, you could keep it. The efforts to snap the apple were the most hilarious, but fishing out the coins was the more rewarding.

Then, around the fire-place, tales were told of Fairies, Ghosts, and Dwarfs. And to see whether there was a good marriage in prospect for a young girl, two half walnut shells were put beside each other close to the fire. If they both flamed up simultaneously, there'd be a good match, if not, a bad one.

The things about Irish culture, aside from literature, which are most familiar and world-famous today – the modernised Gaelic dances of River Dance, or Irish Folk Music with fiddle, hornpipe, whistle, bodhrán, button-accordeon and jew's harp – were in my time certainly not part of daily life, though I naturally don't know what went on in the evening in the pubs and the dance-halls.

The Renaissance of Irish Folk and Irish Dance and the reclaiming of Ireland's extremely rich musical past only started at the end of the 1950s and beginning of the 1960s. At that time we would mostly sing Irish hit-songs, which often had a truly folk-song character: "Rose Of Tralee"; "Hello Patsy Fagan", "I Take The Puff Puff Puff To Ballyjamesduff". I don't know if these are the titles of the songs, or just lines from them. Apart from that, it wasn't just popular music which was in danger of being thoroughly Americanised.

Today it is taken for granted that Céili Dancing is taught in every school, but I saw none of that in my time. Rhythms, at any rate in Jigs and Reels, are deeply embedded in the Irish blood. One particularly shitty rainy Sunday, when I was sitting in the shed with my friend Jack, high up on the hay, he spontaneously began to perform the rhythm of a reel. And, in the absence of words, he used curious sounds, for he couldn't be satisfied just to hum the melody: Nit'n nu, nit'n nit'n nit'n, nat nat nu; Nit'n nu, nit'n nit'n nit'n, nat nat nu. That worked really well and, on top of that, I could rattle along with him in a trice. Even when we see each other today, we don't forget a performance of this makeshift song of our youth.

In our area there was only one man who now and then picked up the Fiddle and played old Irish Melodies: Willy Nally, a relation of my Nallys, who had his farm not to far from ours in Townalough Village. If we sometimes were wandering about near there of an evening, we'd occasionally see Willy sitting alone on the wall outside his house, playing his fiddle. We'd sit down and listen, fascinated, to his melodies.

At the time I intuitively became aware that these Irish sounds belong only in this Irish countryside, with which they merged in a mysterious way. However nice it may be to hear Irish music in Germany on occasion, the original atmosphere of this music can only be experienced in the context of the Irish countryside.

In those days they used to talk about the times when they met in the open at the Cross-roads and music was played for dancing, but this custom no longer survived in my time.

158

41

The Postman

During these two full years at the Nallys, and amidst my friends in Ballinlough and Facefield School, I was only home-sick once, as far as I recall. That was during the monotonous turning of the hay, during which my thoughts wandered towards home and I tried to imagine what things were like there now. I pictured Mother, Father, and Brother Hans, and I know that I cried. Yet my parents always kept me in touch, and every three weeks at least a letter arrived in the spiky handwriting of my father, which I'd have to read out over and over again. In return, Mae, and later Eugene, kept my parents in touch with news.

On account of these letters I knew that my loved ones at home were getting on quite well, probably better than most people in post-War Germany. Shortly after I'd left home and set off for Ireland, my American Aunts succeeded in re-establishing communications with their sisters and their brother. There followed a good supply of Care-Parcels from America, which helped keep their heads above water. So I didn't need to worry about them, and any wish to return home was kept at bay.

Nevertheless the Ballinlough postman was always most eagerly awaited – by Granny or Mae when I was at school. As soon as the Postman was in calling distance he'd shout out "Letter from Germany!" He lived on the mountain on the Kiltimagh Road, which is where our local Post Office was also situated, and he was a weather-beaten man, who was absolutely reliable in storm and rain – and even when 'soaked' inside.

Most of the letters and occasional parcels he delivered would be from America, so people would reward him for prompt delivery – which meant at least one Whiskey in each house.

I see him now, wobbling and weaving back and forth on his bicycle, on that last stretch from the Nevins' to us. He wore a dark blue uniform, and a peaked cap on which the silver emblem of Post Eireann sparkled. During rainy weather he was draped in a heavy, sleeveless oilskin cape. Naturally he'd always get a small mark of appreciation in our place too, which was thankfully consumed with the remark, "But this God-dammed job makes you thirsty".

42

Farewell

One day, coming home from school, an envelope with a Red Cross on it lay on the table. Granny looked at me sadly and pointed at the envelope without a word. To cut a long story short: it was a communication from the Red Cross in Dublin. Numerous German parents, mine among them, had been enquiring about the possibility of bringing their children back to Germany, before the stipulated three years. On account of the considerable numbers, it was practical for the Irish Red Cross to arrange a repatriation transport. More details would be provided in a further letter.

Father had indeed hinted several times that they all longed to see me again and they would be happiest to have me back with them. But to have this actually happen: that didn't suit me at all. To abandon my little Irish paradise, the Nallys, my friends, my neighbours – amongst all of whom I felt so happy. No! That I didn't want. Just five months remained to July 1949, when I was due to leave: surely I could stay on for them. I was dead sad.

But things happen as they must: my departure came at the beginning of February 1949. For the last time I ran down to my village of Ballinlough and said *Tschüss* (cheerio) to all my friends: the Staids, the Nevins, the Regans, the Morans, the Halligans, the Murphys, the McEveneys, the Commons, the Joyces and, and, and.

And every one of them saw me on my way with: "See you again, Herbert, and God bless you!" I shook hands with all my friends a last time at school. I said my goodbyes to Simon and his family in Murneen and to Martin in Belcarra.

The day of my departure was bitterly cold, sunny and crystal-clear. A last look at Croagh Patrick, which seemed to have moved nearer as though he too wanted to say Farewell. Saying goodbye to Granny was really sad and miserable: total despair, masses of tears.

Martin Nevin wanted to bring me to the station in his car, but I didn't want that. If I had to leave, I wanted to cycle to Balla one last time – a journey I'd undertaken so often with my ass-cart, on my bike, and on foot. Eugene came with me.

A last look back: Granny's standing at the gate of the front garden, waving. Major, my dog, who this time made no attempt to run along with us, is sitting on the pillar of the garden-gate and gazing after us. My friend Jack, who'd skived off school to say goodbye, is standing stock still at the corner of our Old House, watching us go. Howling like a hound I push the pedals.

Yet Mayo obviously didn't want to let me go. At Balla Station we find that the train isn't coming for the present. The locomotive is frozen up at Westport. Two hours later, however, it comes puffing up. A painful parting from Eugene – it was 45 years before we were to see each other again.

A Wiedersehen with Mae Nally 2002 in her home in New York. Claire Leydon, nee Nally, Mae's niece, is on the left.

In Dublin I was to report to the Red Cross office – of course I knew my way around the city. When I'd said my piece to the lady in residence, she called out enthusiastically: "Anne, Anne, come here, this boy is a proper Mayo man!" And Anne came running out of the room next door. Both engaged me in a long palaver and were highly delighted and amused at my Mayo accent. My chest swelled and swelled with pride. If these Dubs call me a "Mayo man", then I really am one. And they brought me up to Glencree again, where eventually 30 to 40 German girls and boys were gathered, the absolute majority of whom had no great desire to leave Ireland. Of the unruliness of nearly three years ago, there wasn't a trace.

To my complete amazement Tom Nally and his wife, along with Joe Nally, arrived one day to bid me farewell. My joy was indescribable.

In contrast to our journey to Ireland, the return journey to Germany left little impression. As our steamer beat its way out of Dun Laoghaire Harbour, I went to the stern of the ship and looked back to my Ireland. How poor the country was, with thousands of young people leaving their homeland every year, how spartan and hard the life of the people. Yet what a wealth of human values was native to this nation of the Irish. What exuberant cordiality did I experience, what open-heartedness and attachment, what overwhelming hospitality haven't these Irish afforded,

With parts of my Irish family. From left: Tom, Stephen, Herbert, Claire, Mary, 2000

and not just to me. On this ship, with the country receding ever farther into the distance, I, though just twelve years old, became aware, that in Ireland, in now distant Ballinlough in County Mayo, I have a second home, in which I'm deeply rooted.

43

Home To Cologne

We made a stop in London and I recall that we visited the Tower, and I was loudly reprimanded for calling the uniform of the guards who were strutting about, the Beefeaters, really ridiculous. By the way, we conversed with each other entirely in English.

From Harwich we had an overnight passage in a steamer to the Hook of Holland and were provided with really luxurious and comfortable two-bed cabins.

Yet, by degrees, a feeling of joy about seeing everyone again began to grow, which heightened as our train drew near Cologne. As we draw into the station, we're hanging out of the window, squeezed on top and under each other, and searching in the bustling crowd for parents and brothers and sisters. Then brother Hans is suddenly standing below me at the compartment window:

"Hey, Herbert, don't you know me?"

Then I see Mother and Father as well. Within a few minutes I'm lying in their arms, Mother streaming tears. The first sentence I'm supposed to have said was: *Mutter, weine nicht!* (Mummy, don't cry!)

At home and at school again

I'm stormed with questions and – I understand practically every word. Only answering in my mother-tongue I'm finding difficult. A little while later we're back in our two-room apartment in *Höhenhaus*. I'm home again. *Nun gut,* not so bad!

The greatest adventure and the best time of my childhood were history.

The story
of the cover photo

The story of how an old photograph of children with a donkey cart was reunited with one of those children 60 years later is one of luck and coincidence. I am originally from a small village near Castlebellingham, where Herbert visited and the photograph was taken. A few years ago as I was travelling home from work I decided on a whim to stop at a small restaurant and buy some treats for my wife, who was too pregnant to cook or go out for a meal. While I was waiting, I read the local newspaper, the Drogheda Independent. It had an interesting article about Herbert and his experiences in Ireland. I thought no more about it until some months later. I was visiting a friend in Castlebellingham, Dermot Coyle, who has a small factory there. In his offices, there are some old photographs on the walls, mostly of Castlebellingham in past times. I spotted one photo of children with a donkey cart and I asked him if he knew the background to it. He remembered that the picture had been given him by some elderly friends who had remembered the children visiting after the war. It suddenly struck me that one of these children must be the Herbert in the newspaper article. I contacted the Drogheda Independent, who supplied me with Herbert's details, and the rest, as they say, is history. We sent a copy to Germany, and Herbert was able to spot himself in the picture. How nice it was to connect him with an image of his past.

Stephen Howel

1 The right bank of the Rhine is known to Cologners as the *schäl Sick*, literally 'squinted side'. This is because in old days barge horses walking up river along that bank would have their right eye covered. Central Cologne and the Cathedral are on the left, south-western, bank of the Rhine. The sun shines across from that direction from early noon until late afternoon and would blind the horse's right eye if not covered.

2 The Weimar Republic stimulated self-help Housing Association developments, a new departure in Germany.

3 Allotments were known as *Schrebergärten* called after Dr. Daniel Schreber (1808-1861), who promoted gymnastics and playgrounds.
The allotments movement was founded by a Leipzig headmaster, E. J. Hauschild in 1864.

4 Cologne dialect.

5 Grandma and Grandpa.

6 Esperanto: an auxiliary international language, constructed to foster peace and mutual understanding.

7 Frauentrost Kaffee.

8 Communist Youth: KJVD, Kommunistischer Jugendverband Deutschland. KPD: Kommunistische Partei Deutschlands / Communist Party Deutschland.

9 KZ, Konzentrationslager / Concentration Camp.

10 Geheime Staats Polizei / Secret State Police.

11 30/31 May 1942: Thousand Bomber Raid on Cologne. The RAF Bomber Command Campaign Diary May 1942 reports: "1,047 aircraft were dispatched. The exact number of aircraft claiming to have bombed Cologne is in doubt; the Official History says 898 aircraft bombed but Bomber Command's Night Bombing Sheets indicate that 868 aircraft bombed the main target with 15 aircraft bombing other targets. The total tonnage of bombs was 1,455, two-thirds of this tonnage being incendiaries. German records show that 2,500 separate fires were started, of which the local fire brigade classed 1,700 as large. Property damage in the raid totalled 3,330 buildings destroyed, 2,090 seriously damaged and 7,420 lightly damaged. More than 90 per cent of this damage was caused by fire rather than high-explosive bombs. Among the above total of 12,840 buildings were 2,560 industrial and commercial buildings, though many of these were small ones. However, 36 large firms suffered complete loss of production, 70 suffered 50-80 per cent loss and 222 up to 50 per cent. The estimates of casualties in Cologne are, unusually, quite precise. Figures quoted for deaths vary only between 469 and 486. The 469 figure comprises 411 civilians and 58 military casualties, mostly members of *Flak* units. 5,027 people were listed as injured and 45,132 as bombed out."

12 *"Ach, du leever Jott, Frau Trimborn, Sie sin dat!*

13 *"Jo, Frau Remmel, et nächste mol klääv ich mr e Katzeoog an minge Fott."* / *"Ja und nächstes Mal klebe ich mir ein Katzenauge an meinen Hintern."*

14 *Nationalsozialistische Volkswohlfahrt* / National Socialist People's Welfare.

165

15 *Muckefuck.*

15a The territory Zabrze (Hindenburg) was in dispute between Germany and Poland with armed clashes among German and Polish inhabitants after the Great War. It remained German and the city named Hindenburg until the end of WW II. It now belongs to Poland and is again named Zabrze.

16 Schwaade in Kölsch-Platt.

17 *Altreich.*

18 Meat soaked in vinegar and then roasted.

19 Kölsche Jeck: a real Cologne wag.

20 Winter Help Enterprise.

21 *Kommissbrot*: very tasty non-perishable coarse whole-grain-bread, usually made out of rye, wheat and sourdough. *Kommiss:* in everyday speech the word *Kommiss* is used pejoratively for the German army.

22 *Mülheimer* Boateen: a famous small ferry steam boat crossing on the Rhine, from Mülheim to Cologne, which still operates.

23 *National-Sozialistische Volkswohlfahrt* / National Socialist People's Welfare.

24 *fettes Schwein* = Dekke sau = fat pig.

25 *Schwimmseife* = Floating soap.

26 *"Wenn die Fahrtenmesser blitzen*
und die Hitlerjungen flitzen,
und wir Edelweisspiraten hintendrein.
Was kann das Leben
uns denn noch geben,
Edelweisspiraten wollen wir sein, ja sein".

27 *Ost Wall* = Counterpart to *Westwall* = Siegfried Line.

28 *Volkssturm*: The *"Volkssturm"* consisted mainly of armed older civilian men (> 50 years of age) and youngsters of less than 17 years, unfit to serve in the regular army. The *Volkssturm* was the last army formed, to win a lost war.

29 *Volksgrenadierdivisionen.*

30 *Auf der Heide blüht ein kleines Blümelein.*

31 *Jungvolk*: Nazi youth organisation for youngsters from 10 to 14 years of age, they were called *"Pimpf(e)"*.

32 *Die kumme nit, die driesse sich in de Botz.* Literally: They're shitting their trousers because they are so scared.

33 Have you chocolate, please? Have you chewing gum, please?

34 *Mutterkreuz*, a decoration for mothers introduced in 1938: bronze, silver or gold depending on the number of children.

35 Yes, yes.

36 Carts drawn by panjes, small but very tough Russian horses.

37 There is no 'H' in Russian, and 'G' tends to replace it.

38 "Yes, yes, little Hitler".

39 *"Wenn ich su an ming Heimat denke*
un sinn d'r Dom su vör mir stonn,
mööch ich direck op Heim ahn schwenke,
ich mööch zo Foss noh Kölle jonn".

40 Come on Mrs.! Come on Mrs.!

41 Have you cigarettes? Have you Lucky Strike?

42 *Volksgerichtshof:* notorious People's Court; chief judge Roland Freisler, well-known for his brutal sentences, usually to death.

43 "White and blue come on!"

44 "Here you stay!"

45 "Are you okay?"

46 *"Denn wir fahren gegen Engeland"* (We are sailing against England). A song set to music by Herman Löns (1866-1914). Like the song, *"Bomben auf Engelland"* (Bombs on England), this song was repeatedly played on German radio and was also played during the News Reels *(Wochenschauen)*, making them particularly popular amongst us children. The second verse of Löns' song went something like this:
"Our flag, it waves on the mast, it blazons forth the power of our Reich, for we will no longer stand for the Englishman laughing at it.
(Chorus:) Give me your hand, your white hand; Fare thee well my love, farewell my love, fare well, farewell, because we are moving on England.
Unsre Flagge und die wehet auf dem Maste, sie verkündet unsres Reiches Macht,
denn wir wollen es nicht länger leiden, dass der Englischmann darüber lacht.
(Refrain:) Gib' mir deine Hand, deine weiße Hand,
Leb' wohl, mein Schatz, leb' wohl mein Schatz,
Leb' wohl, lebe wohl, denn wir fahren,
denn wir fahren, denn wir fahren gegen Engelland, Engelland."

47 "Follow me!"

48 "Your name!"

49 "What did you say, Rommel?"

50 "Take them up!"

51 Dropping bombs on England (Engelland is the literary term for England).

52 Your name.

53 Herbert, Herbert, nice name

54 *"Chamberlain, das alte Schwein*
fuhr mi'm Pisspott über den Rhein,
kam er an das Deutsche Eck,
schoss man ihm den Pisspott weg."
Deutsche Eck is at the juncture of the Rhine and Moselle Rivers at Coblenz.

55 Not knowing anything of Anglo-Irish relations then, I was really amazed at how well the verse was received!

56 1620 – Battle in Thirty Years' War on the slopes of the White Mountains near Prague. Ends with the victory of the Catholic League.

57 Hitler utilised a putsch allegedly planned by the SA *(Sturmabteilung /* Storm-troopers, a military organisation of the Nazi party) to wipe out unwanted rivals within the Nazi movement. At least 85 persons were murdered in the so called *"Nacht der langen Messer"* ("night of the long knives") including the leader of the SA, Ernst Röhm.

58 Nazi Germany had a radio station, *Großdeutscher Rundfunk* (Great German Radio), controlled by the Propaganda Ministry (Josef Goebbels).

59 Much, much later – a couple of months before I left to go back to Germany Martin Nevin asked Jack and me to take his cow to a bull which a farmer on the other side of Tawny Lake was keeping illegally. As we were leaving, Martin called after us that we should let the bull perform twice so that there'd be twin calves. So that's what we urged on the owner of the cross-breed – it wasn't listed in any herd-book: "Let him serve twice!" Done as said: and the lusty bull was really able to do it two consecutive times. Back in Germany, one day I got a heartfelt letter from Martin Nevin: "Herbert, you devil, our old cow has twins!

60 In the early 1950s Eugene emigrated to America and we didn't meet again until July 1994 in Ireland. And he confided in me what he hadn't told anyone else: that, during all his years in America, he'd never stopped feeling home-sick for Ballinlough; that he still pined for his work in the fields and on the hay-meadows and on the bog. And, like me, he held a clear recollection of this quite definite day in March 1947, when we ploughed and sowed together. Eugene died in America in December 1994.

61 Blue stone with washing soda.

62 These days – at least near the bigger towns – they are penned into areas set aside for them. And they travel around in large caravans nowadays. Nevertheless, it seems to me that there is more public discrimination against the Tinkers today – at least at the regional level – than there was during my time in Ireland.

63 Again and again Jack and I resolved to climb this mountain, some kilometres from Ballinlough, but we were always too lazy to make the journey. It was not until 1991 that I was able to make this old dream come true. And Baile An Cheo, the "settlement in the mist", as this mountain-village is called, was everything that it promised to be.

64 Goethe Institute: German non-profit organisation whose mission is to promote German language and culture outside Germany and also strengthen Germany's international cultural relations.

Index

171